60 Hikes Within 60 Miles: PORTLAND

60 Hikes Within 60 Miles:

PORTLAND

PAUL GERALD   1st Edition

MENASHA RIDGE PRESS
Birmingham, Alabama

DEDICATION

With immense gratitude and respect, this book is dedicated
to the people who build and maintain trails.

Copyright © 2001 Paul Gerald
All rights reserved
Manufactured in the United States of America
Published by Menasha Ridge Press
Distributed by The Globe Pequot Press
First edition, first printing

Library of Congress Cataloging-in-Publication Data

Gerald, Paul 1966-
  60 hikes within 60 miles, Portland/by Paul Gerald
  p. cm.
  Includes index
  ISBN 0-89732-383-1 (alk. paper)
  1. Hiking—Oregon—Portland Region—Guidebooks. 2. Portland Region (Or.)—
Guidebooks. I. Title: Sixty hikes within sixty miles, Portland. II. Title
GV199.42.O72 P6738 2001
917.95'4904'44—dc21

                                                                  00-068369
                                                                       CIP

Cover and text design by Grant M. Tatum
Cover photo of Mt. Hood by Paul Gerald
Maps by Susanna Fillingham and Steve Jones
Author photo by Cheryl Juetten
All other photos by Paul Gerald

Menasha Ridge Press
P.O. Box 43673
Birmingham, AL 35243
www.menasharidge.com

Table of Contents

Table of Contents (continued)

MAP LEGEND

Main Trail

Alternate Trail

Interstate Highway

U.S. Highway

State Highway

County Road

Forest Service Road

Beachwood Ave.
Local Road

Unpaved Road

Direction of Travel

Appalachian Trail

State Border

County Border

NATIONAL OR STATE
FOREST/PARK

Park-Forest Boundary
and Label

Trailhead
Locator Map

Water Features
Lake/Pond, Creek/River,
and Waterfall

capitol, city, and town

 Mt. Maggie
3,312'

Peaks and Mountains

)€)(€
Footbridge/Dam,
Footbridge, and Dam

❱ ❰
Tunnel

Swamp/Marsh

NORTH

35: Name of Hike

Map Scale

Compass, Map Number,
Name and Scale

◀
Off map or pinpoint
indication arrow

Trailhead
for specific Maps

Ranger Station/
Rest Room Facilities

Ranger Station

Rest Room Facilities

Shelter

Structure
or Feature

Monument/
Sculpture

Parking

Recreation Area

Campgrounds

Picnic Area

vii

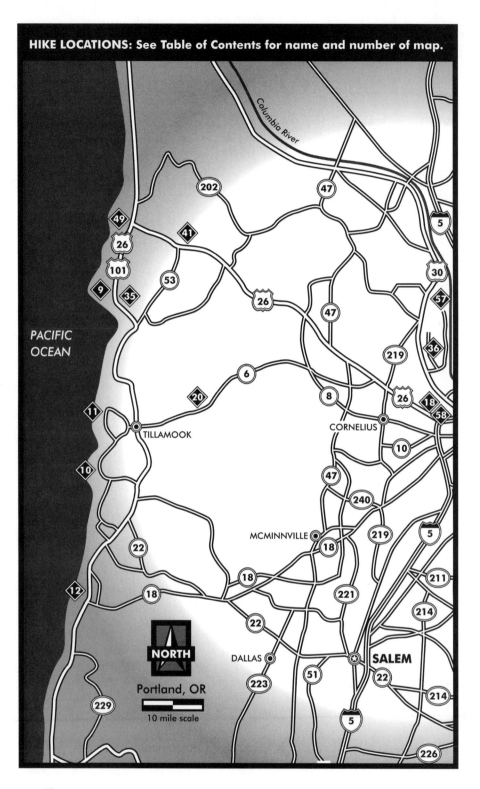

HIKE LOCATIONS: See Table of Contents for name and number of map.

Acknowledgments

Books don't just come from authors. They come from a lot of work by a lot of people. This book wouldn't have happened without the work and assistance of a number of groups and individuals, whom I'd like to thank.

I processed a lot of information for this book, much of which came from the United States Forest Service, Oregon State Parks, the Columbia Gorge Visitors Center, the Mount Hood Visitors Center, The Mazamas, The Crag Rats, and the amazing book *Oregon Geographical Names* from the Oregon Historical Society Press. I own the sixth edition, revised and updated by Lewis L. McArthur, and recommend it highly. Other helpful tidbits and charm came, along the way, from Laurie Mac-Arthur at Opal Creek, Walt Dunn and Carol Wendler at Mount Saint Helens National Volcanic Monument, the "flower ladies" I met on the trail to Paradise Park, and all the nice people at Nature of the Northwest.

The book includes words I wrote, maps I drew, and photographs I took, but many others have put it all together, including Bud Zehmer, Russell Helms, Laura Poole, Annie Long, Carolyn Carroll, Steve Jones, and Susanna Fillingham. Without these folks, the book is just files on my Macintosh.

Thanks and a lunch at McMenamins to Cheryl Juetten for taking the picture of me that's in the back. Thanks and a dinner next time I'm in Rhode Island go to Terre Gorham for applying her legendary editing skills. Also big-time thanks must go to David Lyons and Ed Lawrence for putting me in touch with Menasha Ridge in the first place.

My most personal thanks go to my friends who went hiking with me while I was researching the book. Not only are they good friends and good people, but they all add something wonderful to a walk in the woods. I've put them in alphabetical order, to avoid controversy: Laura Chambers, John and Ümpfa Chandler, Monica Chapin, Christie Dewey, Dana Dister, Craig Frerichs, Tina Henrichson, Brent Kohrt, Jonas Parker, Eliza Rowley, Brandon Rydell, Craig Schumann, Chip Shields, Ladd Van Tol, and Elena Yingling,

And finally, a lifetime of love and thanks to my family back east—Marjorie and Barry Gerald, Lee Gerald, Lucy and Charlie Cook, and their great kids, Rebecca, David, and Jeffrey—and to my family here in Oregon, the Thursday Night Boys.

Foreword

Welcome to Menasha Ridge Press's *60 Hikes Within 60 Miles,* a series designed to provide hikers with information needed to find and hike the very best trails surrounding cities usually underserved by good guidebooks.

Our goal was simple: First, find a hiker who knows the area and loves to hike. Second, ask that person to spend a year researching the most popular and very best trails around. And third, have that person describe each trail in terms of difficulty, scenery, condition, elevation change, and all other categories of information that are important to hikers. "Pretend you've just completed a hike and met up with other hikers at the trailhead," we tell each author. "Imagine their questions; be clear in your answers."

An experienced hiker and writer, author Paul Gerald has selected 60 of his favorite hikes in and around his adopted hometown of Portland. From the civilized hikes of downtown Portland to the rugged trails of volatile Mount St. Helens, Gerald provides hikers (and walkers) with a great variety of trails—and all within 60 miles of Portland.

You'll get more out of this book if you take a moment to read the Introduction explaining how to read the trail listings. The "Maps" section will help you understand how useful topos will be on a hike, and will also tell you where to get them. And since this is a "where-to," not a "how-to" guide, even those of you who have hiked extensively will find the Introduction of particular value.

As much for the opportunity to free the mind as well as to free the body, let Paul Gerald's hikes elevate you above the urban hurry.

All the best.
The editors at Menasha Ridge Press

It's early March in Portland, and the rising sun glows directly behind Mount Hood. Aside from being an inspiring sight—the rays of sun spreading out from behind the mountain, the red glow on the underside of the clouds, the shadow stretching across the city—it's also an inspiring sign. It's confirmation that the sun is moving northward through the sky; warm and dry days are coming, and another hiking season is dawning.

I usually see this wonderful sight from a StairMaster at the YMCA on Barbur Boulevard, where I try to keep my legs and lungs strong over the winter so I can walk up and down hills for the next eight months or so. Sure, you can hike in the winter around here, but who needs it? Short days, muddy trails, rainy skies, few views—I get out there occasionally, because I'm addicted to trails. But the true hiking season starts when that March morning sun rises behind the mountain. That's when I know that very little snow will fall below 3,000 feet, the wildflower show will start in the eastern end of the Columbia River Gorge, the waterfalls will start to go nuclear, and somewhere, up on

Sunrise over Mount Hood and downtown Portland, from Washington Park Rose Garden

a hill or out on a trail, a trillium soon will bloom. And once the trillium blooms, I know there will be no more StairMaster.

The book you're holding is intended to accompany you into the wonderful world that is dayhiking in and around the Portland area. Within these pages are 60 trails that you can hike between breakfast and dinner in the City of Roses. Sixty hikes: At one per week, you've got more than a year of hiking here.

Compared to the pantheon of trails in the area, 60 doesn't seem like much. This corner of America is a hiker's dream, with a wide variety of accessible, well-maintained trails and no shortage of places to find maps, gear, and folks to walk with. But here are 60 select trails which give you a little of everything there is to enjoy around Portland: mountain views, forest solitude, picturesque streams, strenuous workouts, casual strolls, fascinating history, fields of flowers, awesome waterfalls, and ocean beaches.

This book makes it a point to tell you much more than just which direction to go. Think of it as a pack-sized hiking partner, something you can take along to learn from and enjoy as you go. It points out not just which turns to take, but also what to look for along the way. And it strives to educate: Why is Dog Mountain called Dog Mountain? Why are there cables attached to trees along the Clackamas River? Where do all these trails on Lookout Mountain go? What's with that trail above McNeil Point, the one that's not on the official map? Where is the tallest tree in Portland? How do I find the hidden waterfall near the "Throne of the Forest King"?

Even if you've hiked some of these trails before, hiking them with this book will be a new experience for you. And if you've never laced on a pair of hiking boots, or you've just arrived in Portland, here are 60 great places to start. Whether you want a convenient city bus ride to the flat and fascinating Washington Park, a bumpy drive to Lookout Mountain, or the thigh-burning experience that is Mount Defiance, this book will tell you what to bring, how to get to the trailhead, where to go on the trail, and what to look for while you're hiking.

In fact, here's one of my favorite hints—just to get you going—that is not found elsewhere in this book (or any other): When driving to Mount Hood, don't follow the signs that say "Mount Hood." I know that sounds odd, but if you're traveling east on I-84, Exit 16/Mount Hood leads you right through the heart of Gresham, a tangle of strip malls, fast food joints, and traffic lights that only slow you down. Forget that. Take Exit 17/Troutdale, turn right at the second light onto 257th Avenue, and after a couple miles turn left onto SE Orient Road. It will drop you back onto US 26 just one mile before Sandy, after taking you through the kind of country that Gresham replaced: farms, nurseries, country stores, creeks, and a plain two-lane country road. Every time I take people this way, they say two things: First, "Where are we?" and, later, "Man, this is much nicer than the way I usually go."

I suppose that if I am to be your guide, you may want to know some things about me. While hiking has long been one of my favorite activities, I find that when inviting people to come along, I must often assure them that I am not embarking on a major expedition or a speed event. I am, to put it simply, not fast. The hiking times listed in this book are the times I would spend on a trail if I weren't stopping to make notes for a book. But even when I'm not "working," and that's a real stretch of the word, I also stop to eat, drink, look around, relax, take pictures, and eat some more. In other words, I hike to enjoy myself; I go to the YMCA for my workouts. Out on the trail, I average about two miles an hour, with stops included, but the times in the book take into account factors beyond my natural pace: hills, trail condition, altitude, and the number of times needed to stop and say, "Man, look at that (view, waterfall, creek, meadow, etc.)!"

I had hiked more than these 60 trails before I wrote this book, and the toughest decisions I had to make were which hikes to leave out. The range of the book—a rough circle of 60 miles as the crow flies from the edge of the Portland metro area— is bordered on the north by the south side of Mount St. Helens, on the south by Detroit Lake, on the east by OR 35, and on the west by the Pacific Ocean. Hiking these trails, you'll glimpse everything from desert to coastal rainforest, from volcanic aftermath to 1,000-year-old trees.

These things are on my mind when I'm panting on the Stairmaster; all the beauty is out there, just waiting. Maybe, during the winter, we hikers slip out a few times, like when we get a "sunbreak," a word surely made up by weather forecasters in the Pacific Northwest—the same people who distinguish between "rain" and "showers." These "sunbreaks" call us out to the city trails like Forest Park, Washington Park, or the Marquam Trail to Council Crest. Or, we just put on our raincoats to see wild birds in Oaks Bottom or if the steelhead run has made it to Tryon Creek. Sometimes we get tantalizingly clear days, when our eyes glaze over and we say foolish things like, "Is it spring?" Then, we insist on going out to the coast to look for whales from Cape Lookout, into the Gorge to see what Angels Rest is like without 57 other people up there, or down to Silver Falls State Park to see the waterfalls at full blast.

But for the most part, winter is a time to stay in shape at the gym or go play on the snow. March is when the snow starts to melt in lower elevations, especially on

south-facing slopes like the Washington side of the Gorge. March is when you go to Beacon Rock State Park to warm up for Table or Dog Mountains. It's when you find out how well you did in the gym. Or you wallow in the moisture and go see the great waterfalls of the Gorge or hike the Multnomah/Wahkeena loop, Triple Falls, or Eagle Creek before the summer crowds inundate them. Or you drive east of the Rain Shroud, out where it really is spring, to see the wildflowers at McCall Preserve, or stroll the pavement on the Historic Columbia River Highway.

As the snow line rises, so do the hikers. April means you can drive to the Lewis River Trail, or to Siouxon Creek, or to many of the great hikes in the Clackamas and Santiam watersheds—whether it's the old-growth majesty of Opal Creek or the rolling splendor of the Clackamas River itself. April also means there will be Spring Chinook spawning in the Salmon River, and you might even glimpse some in the underwater viewing structure at Wildwood. And when your legs get those early-season blues, there are always the hot springs at Breitenbush and Bagby.

May means the meadows on top of places like Saddle Mountain, Kings Mountain, and Dog Mountain are exploding with flowers—as well as weekend crowds, so steal away on a weekday. It also means those trails just a little farther up are about to be snow-free, and that the roads to places like Lava Canyon, Ape Cave, Ramona Falls, and Larch Mountain will be open.

By June the hiking panorama is practically wide open, and the problem becomes simply where to go. The coast is nice for the duration now, so the views are clear from Tillamook Head and Cape Meares. But back to the east the rhododendrons are blooming on the trails to Salmon Butte, Laurel Hill, Memaloose Lake, and Mirror Lake. You can probably tackle

Shelter atop McNeil Point

south-facing Ape Canyon on the flanks of Mount St. Helens by now, too. And if you really want to see how well you're conditioned, go take a shot at Mount Defiance—and remember, when you're done, there are more hot springs just across the river in Carson.

On July 16, a red-letter date on the hiker's calendar, the road opens to the mind-boggling bluffs of Cascade Head out on the coast. And not long after that the rising temperatures make a splash in Trillium Lake, or one of the Rock Lakes, seem like a good idea.

And then there's August, which to me means one simple thing: wildflowers up high. Every time I arrive in Wy'east Basin, Paradise Park, Elk Meadows, or the ponds below McNeil Point on an August morning, I say to myself, "This is why I live here!" When people in other places say to me, "How can you handle all that rain?" I answer with one word: "August."

In August, it's sunny and around 85 degrees. You're in shape; the meadows on Hood are snow-free and flower-filled; the butterflies are flitting among the blooms; and all is right with the world. And as August yields to September, the sadness is more than made up for by the ripening huckleberries. Anybody who goes for a late-August walk around 5,000 feet elevation in the Pacific Northwest and doesn't move here is either stubborn or insane.

The nice thing about fall is that most people think hiking season is over, so the trails—compared to summer weekends, at least—are practically empty. And September is, in some ways, a sad month, because you know the clear skies are about to end. It feels that way, at least; the truth is that you've still got at least two months before the snows come again, and in the meantime there are the fall colors—the big leaf maples on the Historic Columbia River Highway, the vine maples at Meditation Point on Timothy Lake, and the Mountain Ash on the ridge above Sheep Canyon. The blackberries on the way to Warrior Rock are so numerous you'll think it's an industrial crop,

Middle Falls on the Lewis River

and it's always nice to go back to Silver Falls for a look at the trees and the falls without the throngs of people.

What starts with the sun glowing behind Mount Hood ends with me high up on it. I love the energy of a mountain under threat of winter, and my favorite way to say thanks to the trail gods at the end of the hiking season is to make the long drive to Cloud Cap Saddle, then the long hike to Cooper Spur. I like to sit there with most of the state below me, the October wind blowing a cloud off the summit above me, the Eliot Glacier calving next to me, and about ten of the hikes I've done in my field of vision. I sit there and remember the morning when I was on the StairMaster, looking up at this mountain and saying, "I can't wait to get up there."

Now, I'm there, and it's time to go back down. By early November, the little rock-walled sitting area at the top of Cooper Spur will be under a foot of snow, and I'll pant once more at the gym, or maybe I'll stroll along the Clackamas or in the Gorge, stealing a few more miles of hiking before the first "showers" turn to "rain." Then I'm living for "sunbreaks" once again, dreaming of flowers and butterflies and meadows and waterfalls, watching the rising sun retreat back to the south through the windows of the YMCA.

Paul Gerald

Hiking Recommendations

Hikes Good for Children
3   Ape Cave (lower cave)
26 Lost Lake
37 Oaks Bottom
43 Salmon River (lower portion)
44 Silver Falls State Park
52 Trillium Lake
53 Triple Falls
54 Tryon Creek State Park
58 Washington Park/Hoyt Arboretum
60 Wildwood Recreation Area

Flat Hikes
3   Ape Cave (lower cave)
26 Lost Lake
36 Oak Island
37 Oaks Bottom
43 Salmon River (lower portion)
52 Trillium Lake
54 Tryon Creek State Park
57 Warrior Rock
58 Washington Park/Hoyt Arboretum
60 Wildwood Recreation Area

Steep Hikes
14 Cooper Spur
15 Dog Mountain
20 Kings Mountain
21 Larch Mountain
33 Mount Defiance
34 Mount Mitchell
35 Neahkahnie Mountain
41 Saddle Mountain
47 Table Mountain
56 Wahkeena Falls to Multnomah Falls

Urban Hikes
18 Forest Park
27 Macleay Trail
28 Marquam Trail to Council Crest
37 Oaks Bottom
54 Tryon Creek State Park
58 Washington Park/Hoyt Arboretum

Rural Hikes
7   Breitenbush
9   Cape Falcon
12 Cascade Head
14 Cooper Spur
33 Mount Defiance
38 Opal Creek
40 Rock Lakes
42 Salmon Butte
45 Siouxon Creek
46 South Fork Toutle River

Secluded Hikes
8   Bull of the Woods
14 Cooper Spur
31 Memaloose Lake
34 Mount Mitchell
40 Rock Lakes
45 Siouxon Creek
47 Table Mountain
55 Vista Ridge
59 Whetstone Mountain

Hikes Good for Wildlife Watching
10 Cape Lookout State Park
11 Cape Meares
12 Cascade Head

17 Elk Meadows
27 Macleay Trail
36 Oak Island
37 Oaks Bottom
43 Salmon River
57 Warrior Rock
60 Wildwood Recreation Area

21 Larch Mountain
22 Laurel Hill
23 Lava Canyon
27 Macleay Trail
38 Opal Creek
46 South Fork Toutle River
49 Tillamook Head
57 Warrior Rock

Scenic Hikes

9 Cape Falcon
10 Cape Lookout State Park
12 Cascade Head
14 Cooper Spur
16 Eagle Creek
17 Elk Meadows
21 Larch Mountain
25 Lookout Mountain
30 McNeil Point
46 South Fork Toutle River
55 Vista Ridge

Trails Featuring Waterfalls

16 Eagle Creek
21 Larch Mountain
23 Lava Canyon
24 Lewis River
39 Ramona Falls
44 Silver Falls State Park
45 Siouxon Creek
48 Tamanawas Falls
53 Triple Falls
56 Wahkeena Falls to Multnomah Falls

In the following categories, parentheses indicate a shorter option within a longer hike.

Trails Good for Runners

10 Cape Lookout State Park
13 Clackamas River
18 Forest Park
19 Historic Columbia River Highway
26 Lost Lake
27 Macleay Trail
28 Marquam Trail to Council Crest
42 Salmon Butte
51 Timothy Lake
52 Trillium Lake

Less than 1 mile

3 Ape Cave (lower cave)
11 Cape Meares (to lighthouse, Octopus Tree, or Big Spruce)
18 Forest Park (several options)
22 Laurel Hill (to chute or Little Zigzag Falls)
23 Lava Canyon (upper loop)
24 Lewis River (to Lower Falls)
36 Oak Island
44 Silver Falls State Park (South Falls Loop)
50 Timberline Lodge (to White River Canyon overlook)
51 Timothy Lake (to Little Crater Lake)
53 Triple Falls (to Ponytail Falls)
54 Tryon Creek State Park (several options)
58 Washington Park/Hoyt Arboretum (several options)
60 Wildwood Recreation Area

Multi-Use Trails

5 Barlow Pass
18 Forest Park
19 Historic Columbia River Highway
22 Laurel Hill
25 Lookout Mountain
38 Opal Creek
40 Rock Lakes

Historic Trails

6 Beacon Rock State Park
14 Cooper Spur
19 Historic Columbia River Highway

Introduction

Welcome to *60 Hikes within 60 Miles: Portland!* If you're new to hiking or even if you're a seasoned trail-smith, take a few minutes to read the following introduction. We explain how this book is organized and how to use it.

Hike Descriptions

Each hike contains six key items: a locator map, an In Brief description of the trail, an At-a-Glance Information box, directions to the trail, a trail map, and a hike narrative. Combined, the maps and information provide a clear method to assess each trail from the comfort of your favorite chair.

Locator Map

After narrowing down the general area of the hike on the overview map (see pp. viii–ix), the locator map, along with driving directions given in the narrative, enables you to find the trailhead. Once at the trailheads, park only in designated areas.

In Brief

This synopsis of the trail offers a snapshot of what to expect along the trail, including mention of any historical sights, beautiful vistas, or other interesting sights you may encounter.

At-a-Glance Information

The At-a-Glance Information boxes give you a quick idea of the specifics of each hike. There are 13 basic elements covered.

Length The length of the trail from start to finish. There may be options to shorten or extend the hikes, but the mileage corresponds to the described hike. Consult the hike description to help decide how to customize the hike for your ability or time constraints.

Configuration A description of what the trail might look like from overhead. Trails can be loops, out-and-backs (that is, along the same route), figure eights, or balloons. Sometimes the descriptions might surprise you.

Difficulty The degree of effort an "average" hiker should expect on a given hike. For simplicity, difficulty is described as "easy," "moderate," or "hard."

Scenery Rates the overall environs of the hike and what to expect in terms of plant life, wildlife, streams, or historic buildings.

Exposure A quick check of how much sun you can expect on your shoulders during the hike. Descriptors used are self-explanatory and include terms such as shady, exposed, and sunny.

Traffic Indicates how busy the trail might be on an average day. Trail traffic, of course, will vary from day to day and season to season.

Trail surface Indicates whether the trail is paved, rocky, smooth dirt, or a mixture of elements.

Hiking time How long it took the author to hike the trail. Paul says he makes about two miles an hour—a little quicker if it's flat, a little slower if it's steep. He can go faster, but he sees little reason to do so. Hiking, after all, is supposed to be fun. The gym is for exercise.

Season Times of year when this trail is accessible. In most cases, the limiting factor is snow on the trail or the road to the trailhead, but in some cases trails are closed for reasons relating to wildlife habitat. In any case, if it's a border time for the trail you want to hike, call the information number to be sure you can hike it.

Access Notes fees or permits needed to access the trail. Most Portland-vicinity trailheads on National Forest or National Monument lands require the Northwest Forest Pass, which can be obtained at many local outdoor shops and also at any Forest Service ranger station or information station. A day pass is $5, an annual pass is $30. For more information about the Pass, call (800) 270-7504.

Maps Which map is the best, in the author's opinion, for this hike. See Appendix B for places to buy maps.

Facilities Notes any facilities such as rest rooms, phones, and water available at the trailhead or on the trail.

Special comments Provides you with those little extra details that don't fit into any of the above categories. Here you'll find information on trail hiking options and facts such as whether or not to expect a lifeguard at a nearby swimming beach.

Directions

Check here for directions to the trailhead. Used with the locator map, the directions will help you locate each trailhead.

Description

The trail description is the heart of each hike. Here, the author has provided a summary of the trail's essence as well as highlighted any special traits the hike offers. Ultimately the hike description will help you choose which hikes are best for you.

Nearby Activities

Not every hike will have this listing. For those that do, look here for information on nearby dining opportunities or other activities to fill out your day.

Weather

For most folks, hiking season around Portland starts in March or April, when flowers and temperatures start to rise. Unfortunately, that's the least stable of seasons where the weather is concerned. Weather forecasts are notoriously off the mark during spring, so if they aren't absolutely, positively sure it will be clear, plan for 50-something and drizzling into June.

Snow is a different matter; the higher hikes in this book won't be completely clear until July most years. Also beware that in the Columbia River Gorge, wind is a constant reality, so even a sunny June day on a hike like Dog Mountain can have you reaching for hat and gloves. By mid to late June, and all the way into October, you'll see mostly sunny skies, mild temperatures, and happy hikers. Then winter comes and, for all intents and purposes, it rains until spring. We try to think of it as waterfall-loading.

Average Daily (High) Temperatures by Month
Portland, Oregon

Jan	Feb	Mar	Apr
46	51	56	61
May	**Jun**	**Jul**	**Aug**
68	74	80	81
Sep	**Oct**	**Nov**	**Dec**
75	64	53	46

Maps

The maps in this book have been produced with great care and, used with the hiking directions, will help you stay on course. But as any experienced hiker knows, things can get tricky off the beaten path.

The maps in this book, when used with the route directions present in each chapter, are sufficient to get you to the trail and keep you on it. However, you will find superior detail and valuable information in the United States Geological Survey's 7.5 minute series topographic maps (topos). Recognizing how indispensable these are to hikers and bikers alike, many outdoor shops and bike shops now carry topos of the local area.

If you're new to hiking, you might be wondering, "What's a topographic map?" In short, these differ from standard "flat" maps, indicating not only linear distance but elevation as well. One glance at a topo will show you the difference: Contour lines spread across the map like dozens of intricate spider webs. Each contour line represents a particular elevation, and at the base of each topo a particular contour interval designation is given. Yes, it sounds confusing if you're new to the lingo, but it truly is a simple and wonderfully helpful system.

Let's assume that the 7.5 minute series topo reads "Contour Interval 40 feet," that the short trail we'll be hiking is two inches in length on the map, and that it crosses five contour lines from its beginning to end. What do we know? Well, because the linear scale of this series is 2,000 feet to the inch (roughly two and three-quarters inches representing one mile), we know our trail is approximately four-fifths of a mile long (2 inches are 2,000 feet). But we also know we'll be climbing or descending 200 vertical feet (5 contour lines are 40 feet each) over that distance. And the elevation designations written on occasional contour lines will tell us if we're heading up or down.

In addition to outdoor shops and bike shops, you'll find topos at major universities and some public libraries, where you might try photocopying the ones you need to avoid the cost of buying them. But if

you want your own and can't find them locally, contact:

USGS Map Sales
Box 25286
Denver, CO 80225
(888) ASK-USGS(275-8747)
www.mapping.usgs.gov/esic/

Visa and MasterCard are accepted. Ask for an index while you're at it, plus a price list and a copy of the booklet Topographic Maps. In minutes you'll be reading topos like a pro.

A second excellent series of maps available to hikers is distributed by the United States Forest Service. If your trail runs through an area designated as a national forest, look in the phone book under the United States Government listings, find the Department of Agriculture heading, and run your finger down that section until you find the Forest Service. Give them a call, and they'll provide the address of the regional Forest Service office, from which you can obtain the appropriate map.

Trail Etiquette

Whether you're on a city walk or on a long hike, always remember that great care and resources (from nature as well as from your tax dollars) have gone into creating these trails. Taking care of the trails begins with you, the hiker. Treat the trail, wildlife, and your fellow hikers with respect. Here are a few general ideas to keep in mind while hiking.

1. Hike on open trails only. Respect trail and road closures (ask if you're not sure), avoid trespassing on private land, and obtain permits and authorization as may be required.

2. Leave no trace of your visit other than footprints. Be sensitive to the dirt beneath you. This also means staying on the trail and not creating any new ones. Be sure to pack out what you pack in. No one likes to see trash someone else has left behind.

3

3. Never spook animals. Give animals extra room and time to adjust to you. Leave gates as you found them or as marked.

4. Plan ahead. Know your equipment, your ability, and the area in which you are hiking—and prepare accordingly. Be self-sufficient at all times; carry necessary supplies for changes in weather or other conditions. A well-executed trip is a satisfaction to you and not a burden or offense to others.

5. Be courteous to other hikers, or bikers, you meet on the trails.

Water

"How much is enough? One bottle? Two? Three?! But think of all that extra weight!" Well, one simple physiological fact should convince you to err on the side of excess when it comes to deciding how much water to pack: While working hard in 90-degree heat, we each need approximately 10 quarts of fluid every day. That's 2.5 gallons—12 large water bottles or 16 small ones. And, with water weighing in at approximately 8 pounds per gallon, a one-day supply comes to a whopping 20 pounds.

In other words, pack along one or two bottles even for short hikes. And make sure you can purify the water found along the trail on longer routes. If you drink it untreated, you run the risk of disease.

Many hikers pack along the inexpensive and only slightly distasteful tetraglycine hydroperiodide tablets (sold under the names Potable Aqua, Globaline, and Coughlan's, among others). If you wait for these tablets to work their magic, usually about 30 minutes, and then add a few grains of vitamin C powder, your water will instantly clear up again. Some invest in portable, lightweight purifiers that filter out the crud. Unfortunately, even the best filters only remove up to 98–99% of all those nasty bacteria, viruses, and other organisms you can't see.

Tablets or iodine drops by themselves will knock off the well-known Giardia. One to four weeks after ingestion, Giardia will have you bloated, vomiting, shivering with chills, and living in the bathroom. But there are other parasites to worry about, including cryptosporidium. "Crypto" brings on symptoms very similar to Giardia, but unlike that fellow protozoan it's equipped with a shell sufficiently strong to protect it against the chemical killers that stop Giardia cold. This means either boiling the water or using a water filter to screen out both Giardia and crypto, plus the iodine to knock off viruses.

Some water filters come equipped with an iodine chamber to guarantee nearly full protection. Or you can simply add a pill or drops to the water you've just filtered (if you aren't allergic to iodine, of course). The pleasures of hiking—and the displeasure of getting sick—make this relatively minor effort worth every one of the few minutes involved.

First-Aid Kit

A typical kit may contain more items than you might think necessary. But these are just the basics. Pack the items in a waterproof bag such as a Ziploc bag or a similar product.

Sunscreen
Aspirin or acetaminophen
Butterfly-closure bandages
Band-Aids
Snakebite kit
Gauze (one roll)
Gauze compress pads (a half-dozen
    4 in. x 4 in.)
Ace bandages or Spenco joint wraps
Benadryl or the generic equivalent—
    diphenhydramine (an antihistamine,
    in case of allergic reactions)

A prefilled syringe of epinephrine (for those known to have severe allergic reactions to such things as bee stings)

Water purification tablets or water filter (on longer hikes)

Moleskin/Spenco "Second Skin"

Hydrogen peroxide or iodine

Antibiotic ointment (Neosporin or the generic equivalent)

Matches or pocket lighter

Whistle (more effective in signaling rescuers than your voice)

Hiking with Children

No one is too young for a nice hike in the woods or through a city park. Parents with infants can strap the little ones on with devices such as the Baby-Björn Baby Carrier® or Kelty's Kangaroo®. Be careful, though. Flat, short trails are probably best with an infant. Toddlers who have not quite mastered walking can still tag along, riding on an adult's back in a child carrier.

Children who are walking can, of course, follow along with an adult. Use common sense to judge a child's capacity to hike a particular trail. Always rely on the possibility that the child will tire quickly and have to be carried.

When packing for the hike, remember the child's needs as well as your own. Make sure children are adequately clothed for the weather, have proper shoes, and are properly protected from the sun with sunscreen and clothing. Kids dehydrate quickly, so make sure you have plenty of clean water and other drinks for everyone.

Depending on age, ability, and the hike length/difficulty, most children should enjoy the shorter hikes described in this book. To assist an adult with determining which trails are suitable for children, a list of hike recommendations for children is provided on page xix.

The Business Hiker

Whether you're in the Portland area on business as a resident or visitor, these hikes are the perfect opportunity to make a quick getaway from the demands of commerce. Many of the hikes are classified as urban and are easily accessible from downtown areas.

Instead of a burger down the street, pack a lunch and head out to one of the area's many urban trails for a relaxing break from the office or that tiresome convention. Or plan ahead and take a small group of your business comrades on a nearby hike in one of the area forests. A well-planned half-day getaway is the perfect complement to a business stay in Portland.

60 Hikes Within 60 Miles:

PORTLAND

Angels Rest

Columbia River

84

Historic Columbia River Hwy.

1

To Portland

Exit 28 (Bridal Veil)

IN BRIEF

There's a reason they recently expanded the parking area for this one: it's one of the finer hikes around, with a gentle grade to a spectacular lookout point above the Columbia River. It also connects with the Wahkeena Trail, making longer loops or one-way hikes with shuttles possible.

DIRECTIONS

From Portland on Interstate 84, drive 21 miles east of Interstate 205 to Exit 28/ Bridal Veil. After less than a mile, park in the sprawling parking area at the intersection with the Historic Columbia River Highway. The signed trailhead is just across the old highway.

DESCRIPTION

As you drive out Interstate 84, you can actually see Angels Rest, a flat-topped rock outcropping sticking out over the road at the end of a ridge. What looks like a building on top is actually a clump of trees. And if it looks like it's way up there, just remember that if you take your time on the way up you'll have plenty of breath left to be taken away by the view up top.

The trail starts with a moderate climb through the woods and has an early reward: a rare view down at a waterfall, in this case 100-foot Coopey Falls. Soon thereafter, the trail crosses Coopey Creek on a wooden bridge and then starts climbing just a little more steeply.

KEY AT-A-GLANCE INFORMATION

Length:
4.6 miles

Configuration:
Out-and-back

Difficulty:
Moderate, due to altitude gain and a little rock scrambling at the top

Scenery:
Forest most of the way, waterfall, creek crossing, panorama at the top

Exposure:
Shady except for one section

Traffic:
Heavy; on a nice weekend day this trail will have more dogs on it than many trails have hikers.

Trail surface:
Packed dirt with some roots, rocks

Hiking time:
2.5 hours

Season:
Year-round

Access:
No fees or permits needed

Maps:
Trails of the Columbia Gorge; Green Trails #428 (Bridal Veil); USGS Bridal Veil

Facilities:
Rest rooms and water one-half mile west at Bridal Veil State Park

Columbia River

To
Multnomah
Falls

Historic Columbia
River Hwy.

84

To
Wahkeena
Trail

Angels Rest
1560'

Coopey
Falls

Rockslide

P

1

P

150'

Coopey
Creek

To
Portland

NORTH

1: Angels Rest

0.5 mile scale

After about a mile, you'll start switching back through an area that burned in 1991; note the blackened trunks of some of the bigger trees. It was mostly just the underbrush and smaller trees that burned, opening up the forest floor to the sun and letting wildflowers come in to take your mind off the climb. When the trail traverses a rock slide for 100 yards, you're almost done.

Just past the slide, the trail goes back into the woods briefly, and you turn left out onto the final ridge. This last stretch of the trail is why you might think twice about bringing small children: It gets a little narrow, with cliffs to the east falling away a few hundred feet, and in one spot you'll have to scramble up about ten feet of rocks. When a trail goes off to the right on the ridge top, stay straight.

The reward for this small effort is a view to rival any other in the Gorge. To the east, you can see Beacon Rock and the high walls on either side of the river. To the west you can see the Vista House and the hills falling away toward Portland and the Willamette Valley. The Columbia River, right below you, seems so close that you could get a running start and jump into it. You might see some windsurfers out there; on one trip, I watched a float plane practicing touch-and-go landings on this stretch of the river. All in all, it's hard to imagine a better place to have lunch.

If you're up for more hiking, you can turn this into a longer loop or do a one-way hike with another car parked farther east. To do this, as you walk back down the ridge, veer left (east) instead of keeping straight, which is where you came from. After a few minutes you'll come to a junction; go left to head for the Wahkeena Trail.

In 2.5 miles you'll come to Wahkeena Spring, and 0.1 mile later you'll intersect the Wahkeena Trail (#420). Here, you can turn left (downhill) and follow Wahkeena Creek 1.6 miles down to the picnic area at Wahkeena Falls, or you can go straight and, in 1.2 miles, intersect the Larch Mountain Trail. Go down that one for 1.8 miles, and you'll be at Multnomah Falls.

NEARBY ACTIVITIES

The Vista House, as well as the road that leads to it, is well worth a visit. To get there, simply drive back toward Portland on the Historic Highway, rather than on Interstate 84. Follow the 85-year-old road and its moss-covered stone guardrails past a few other waterfalls and then up the hill to Crown Point, where you can step into the Vista House and get yourself an espresso while you take in a postcard view and historic displays about the building of the road. Keep going west on that road past the Vista House, and in a couple of miles you'll see a sign leading you down a steep hill back to Interstate 84.

Ape Canyon

IN BRIEF

This trail visits two worlds not ordinarily seen: the upper reaches of a volcano and the edge of what they call the "blast zone." Without too much climbing, you can stand in a wonderful old-growth forest and be about 20 feet from an area that was completely obliterated barely 20 years ago. At the top, you'll have a sweeping view highlighted by an amazing geological oddity.

DIRECTIONS

From Portland on Interstate 5, drive 21 miles north of the Columbia River and take Exit 21/Woodland. Turn right onto Washington Highway 503 (Lewis River Road), which after 31 miles (2 miles past the town of Cougar) turns into Forest Service Road 90. Follow FS 90 for 3.3 miles and turn left onto FS 83. The trailhead is 11.2 miles ahead on the left, just before the Lava Canyon trailhead.

DESCRIPTION

You'll get your first glimpse of the contrasts ahead when you've only walked 100 yards on this trail. You'll be at the top of a little bluff, looking out over a wide area of rocks. Those rocks used to be on the upper slopes of the volcano Mount St. Helens, but on May 18, 1980, they came down the hill at about 45 miles per hour, part of a landslide triggered when most of the Shoestring Glacier melted in a moment when the

KEY AT-A-GLANCE INFORMATION

Length:
11.6 miles

Configuration:
Out-and-back

Difficulty:
Moderate

Scenery:
Old-growth forest, a volcanic mudflow, a narrow canyon

Exposure:
Alternating shady and open on the way up, then wide open at the top

Traffic:
Moderate on summer weekends, light otherwise

Trail surface:
Packed dirt with roots and rocks, rock at the top

Hiking time:
5.5 hours

Season:
June through October

Access:
Northwest Forest Pass required

Maps:
USFS Mount St. Helens National Volcanic Monument

Facilities:
None at trailhead; toilets at Lava Canyon trailhead. There's no water at the trailhead or on the trail.

Plains of
Abraham

Loowit
Trail

Ape Canyon
Viewpoint

NORTH

2: Ape Canyon

1 mile scale

Loowit
Trail

Ape Canyon
Trail

2

P

Muddy
Creek

FS 83

volcano erupted. But the mudslide stayed within the boundaries of the Muddy River, so the forest you're standing in—even though it was within feet of the slide—was spared. You'll spend the next 5 miles climbing this ridge, but don't worry: you'll only gain a little more than 1,300 feet along the way.

Before you leave this viewpoint, look down. You're standing on an example of stratigraphy; that's a fancy word for the fact that when the 1980 mudflow came through, it exposed several underlying layers of rock, which give scientists clues to the previous eruption history of the volcano.

If you're on this trail in September or October, you'll be in the world of the vine maple, whose red and orange explosion contrasts beautifully with the evergreen canopy. Keep an eye out for deer and elk, both of which are in the area. You won't see old-growth forest for about a mile and a half, but when you do you'll see some monster hemlocks. At this elevation they tend to get quite fat

South side of Mt. Saint Helens, showing the lahar (mudflow) damage from 1980

at the base but not as tall as usual, due to violent winter storms. Soon after you enter the old growth and climb some switchbacks, you'll get views out to the east of Mount Adams, the second highest peak in Washington at 12,276 feet. It's about 35 miles away. Mount Hood, 60 miles away to the south, is also visible, as is Mount Rainier to the north.

After five miles of gradual climbing, you'll come out into the open—and into the "blast zone" itself. You'll see trees that were killed by the super-heated gases produced when the mountain blew in 1980, and to the north (ahead of you) you will see the utter desolation the eruption created. (The explosion was actually "aimed" that way.)

When you come to a lookout point on the right, you can scramble down a bit (be very careful) and look into the 300-foot slot that lies at the head of Ape Canyon, which now stretches away to

your right. If you work it right, it makes a heck of a foreground for a picture of Mount Adams. It's also visible from a little farther up the trail.

Just beyond this point, there's an intersection with the Loowit Trail, which goes all the way around Mount St. Helens. To your left, up a small rise, is an excellent viewpoint back down the mudflow toward your car. If you turn right and go 0.8 mile up the Loowit Trail, you'll come to the Plains of Abraham, which might as well have been lifted from the moon.

If you're wondering about the name of this hike, it comes from a 1920s incident in which an ape-like "Bigfoot" (decades later found to be a kid playing a prank) threw rocks at some miners in the area. The only connection between Ape Canyon and Ape Cave is in the name; Ape Cave was discovered by the Mount St. Helens Apes, who took their name

from the Ape Canyon legend. For more
information, contact the Mount St.
Helens National Volcanic Monument
office at (360) 247–3900.

NEARBY ACTIVITIES
If you'd like an even more dramatic view
of the blast zone from the eruption of
Mount St. Helens, drive around to the
Windy Ridge Visitor Center, northeast of
the mountain in the heart of the scene of
destruction. In the summer, rangers give
talks every hour on the half hour. To get
there, when you get back to FS 90, turn
left, and follow the signs; it's about 55
paved miles from there.

Top of Ape Canyon
with Mt. Adams in the background

Ape Cave

IN BRIEF

If you've ever wanted to go caving, this is a great chance. You have two options: One is an easy stroll with plenty of room; the other is more challenging and requires a little climbing here and there. Both are fun and fascinating for the whole family. Also, forest rangers lead hikes into the cave, so call ahead for that schedule.

DIRECTIONS

From Portland on Interstate 5, drive 21 miles north of the Columbia River and take Exit 21/Woodland. Turn right onto Washington Highway 503 (Lewis River Road), which after 31 miles (2 miles past the town of Cougar) turns into FS 90. Follow FS 90 for 3.3 miles and turn left onto FS 83. Go 1.6 miles and turn left onto FS 8303, following a sign for Ape Cave. The well-marked trailhead is 0.9 mile ahead.

DESCRIPTION

This is no ordinary hike, to be sure, but it's something everyone should see. Even if you're claustrophobic and afraid of the dark, you should be able to handle the lower cave, which in the world of caving is a walk in the park.

Where did this cave come from? Technically it's a lava tube (the longest one in the continental United States), left behind after an eruption of Mount St. Helens 1,900 years ago. Lava on the surface

KEY AT-A-GLANCE INFORMATION

Length:
Lower cave is 1.6 miles round-trip; upper cave is 2.3 miles round-trip. Access trail adds 0.4 mile to both

Configuration:
Lower, out-and-back; upper, loop

Difficulty:
Lower cave, easy; upper, hard

Scenery:
Inside of a lava tube, with cave features and dripping water

Exposure:
None

Traffic:
Use is heavy all summer, especially in the lower cave.

Trail surface:
Pavement on the access trail; rock, packed dirt

Hiking time:
1 hour for lower cave; 3 hours for upper cave

Season:
May through October

Access:
Northwest Forest Pass required

Maps:
USFS Mount St. Helens National Volcanic Monument

Facilities:
Rest rooms at the trailhead

Cave Exit
2,480'

Skylight

Return Trail
On Surface

Lava
Falls

NORTH

3: Ape Cave

0.5 mile scale

Upper
Cave

Cave
Entrance
2,080'

3

P

FS 83

Lower
Cave

Meatball

FS 8303

Trail of
2 Forests

To FS 90

cooled, but it kept running underneath, and when it was gone the tube was left behind. Since then, other eruptions have filled the bottom, making a nice floor to walk on, and earthquakes have shaken boulders loose from the ceiling of the upper cave. In places, you can make out ripple marks on the floor where lava cooled in waterlike patterns.

Now, as for the name. There are, of course, no apes here. A local band of Boy Scouts took that name from a legendary (and staged) Bigfoot sighting in the 1920s. That "sighting" took place in what's now called Ape Canyon. The Scouts found the cave; hence, Ape Cave.

After walking a paved 0.2-mile trail from the parking lot, you'll arrive at the main entrance to the cave. Walk down the stone steps and pause to give your eyes some time to adjust. Even your flashlight beacon will seem very dim at first. Walk down a set of metal steps, and when you get to the bottom the lower cave will be in front of you. The upper cave starts behind the steps. Do the lower cave first.

As you walk along, look out for features such as "sand castles." Over the centuries before people came along, water washed away most of the sand on the floor but left some "castles" standing. Because there was no wind, they stood there for hundreds of years, until people came along and knocked most of them over. There are a few left, though, so watch your step. Also look along the ceiling for "lava-sicles," which look like tiny stalactites but were formed differently.

Stalactites are formed by dripping water, but these resulted when superheated gases melted parts of the cave ceiling, which then dripped down to form lava-sicles.

Another thing that happened was that as the cave cooled, pieces of it broke off as large rocks and flowed with the lava. One of these pieces, known as "the meatball," was left wedged ten feet over your head toward the end of the cave.

A really fun thing to do, especially in the lower cave, is to stand still and turn off your light when you hear somebody coming. For one thing, you get a real appreciation of true darkness; your eyes won't adjust, because there is no light to adjust to. But it is cool to watch the lights of the other party approach through the cave, and lanterns make some incredibly funny-looking shadows on the walls. Just turn your light back on before they reach you, or you might spook them.

Eventually, 0.8 mile from the start, the lower cave ends when the ceiling simply becomes too low to continue and pinches down to nothing. This happens because here the tube dips downhill, and the mudflow that made the floor so easy to walk on filled up the whole thing.

Now, for the upper cave. Less than 100 yards beyond the steps, you'll come to a big pile of rocks that you have to climb over; get used to it. In the next 1.4 miles, which will probably take you more than 2 hours, there are about a dozen of these rock piles. One thing should set you at ease, though: There is only one cave here, so even if you're up on a pile of boulders and briefly lose your sense of direction, you won't get lost.

Look for the same features here as described for the lower cave, with two additions. At just under a mile, you'll have to climb up two waterfalls of lava. The second one is a particular challenge. Somebody chipped a foothold into it a few feet off the floor, but after that you're on your own. The lava offers good traction, though, so trust that your shoes will hold. The best advice is to put your left foot in the hold, brace your right foot against the far wall, then put your hands on the rock and push up. Rock climbers might call this a chimney move followed by a mantle, but it's not as tough as it sounds.

A little ways past this point you'll come under a skylight, which is too high to climb out of, but when you get there you've only got 0.3 mile to go. At the end, a metal ladder on the left leads out into the world again, and the trail is an easy, downhill stroll of 1.2 miles back to the main entrance.

NEARBY ACTIVITIES

For another look at the area's geological history, stop at the boardwalk Trail of Two Forests on the way back to FS 83. Here, the same eruption that created Ape Cave engulfed a forest, leaving 1,900-year-old tree molds in the lava.

Bagby Hot Springs

IN BRIEF

Unless you've got issues about being among naked people, this is one place you should positively visit. The hike isn't much of a challenge, but the destination is sublime: historic hot springs with cedar-log tubs, some of them private, surrounded by ancient-growth forest.

DIRECTIONS

From Portland on Oregon Highway 224, travel 44 miles southeast of Interstate 205, through the town of Estacada, to the ranger station at Ripplebrook. Turn right onto FS 46 and, 3.6 miles later, right again onto FS 63. Travel 3.5 miles and turn right onto FS 70. The trailhead is six miles ahead on the left.

DESCRIPTION

It seems everybody in the area knows about Bagby, even the folks who haven't actually been there. Just the word seems to stand for something about life in the Pacific Northwest: soothing, relaxing, a retreat from the hustle-and-bustle world, back into the days of the ancient forest and natural elements.

Well it's not just that. A nonprofit group called Friends of Bagby has built two bathhouses on the property, and the chances you'll be the only people there are slim. On weekends you might have to wait to soak, unless you start early.

From the trailhead parking lot, start up the wide trail (an expressway by normal

KEY AT-A-GLANCE INFORMATION

Length:
3 miles round-trip to the springs

Configuration:
Out-and-back

Difficulty:
Easy

Scenery:
Old-growth forest, a mountain stream, and tubs of hot water

Exposure:
Shady all the way

Traffic:
Use is quite heavy.

Trail surface:
Packed dirt with some muddy spots in winter and spring

Hiking time:
1 hour round-trip (with hot soak)

Season:
Year-round, but it does get some snow, so call ahead for conditions.

Access:
Northwest Forest Pass required

Maps:
USGS Bagby Hot Springs; USFS Bull of the Woods Wilderness

Facilities:
Toilets at the trailhead and at the springs, but no water. The water in streams along the hike must be treated.

NORTH

4: Bagby Hot Springs

0.5 mile scale

Nohorn Creek

FS 70

P

4

Hot
Springs
Fork

Peggy
Creek

Hot
Springs

Campsites →

Shower
Creek

trail standards) and cross a bridge over Nohorn Creek, named after the nick-name of an early pioneer in the area. The hiking is pleasant, the pools in the river inviting, and the forest inspiring. If you happen to notice some old metal loops tacked high into the trees, those once held telephone wires that connect-ed fire lookouts back in the 1930s. When you cross a bridge over Hot Springs Fork, you're almost to the springs.

When you come to the springs area, the first thing you'll notice is the 1913 ranger cabin, which is listed on the National Register of Historic Places. It was a central communications station for those fire lookouts. I should mention that this cabin of 16-inch cedar logs was hand-built by one ranger, a certain Phil Putz, who first visited the area after walking 39 miles in one day. You think he was happy to find the springs? The path behind the cabin leads to a monumental downed tree; check out the inside, which was rotted away long before the giant was cut to keep it from squashing the bathhouses.

The bathhouse on the right has one big tub, with room for five or six adults. The one on the left has an open area with several tubs and five private rooms, each with a two-person log tub. The water comes out of the springs at 136 degrees and runs through a system of log flumes. To fill a tub, you just open up the valve and let the hot water in, then grab a bucket, fill it with cold water from a nearby tub, and get the temperature where you want it. Typically, a full tub needs four or five buckets of cold water to make it tolerable. As it cools off, just open up the valve and let some more hot stuff in. It's fantastic. Friends of Bagby says that about 50% of bathers don't wear suits, but in areas other than the tubs it's asked that you do wear clothing. They also ask that if people are waiting you limit your soaking to one hour.

Even if there's nobody around when you get to the springs, consider taking some time to explore farther up the trail before you soak. It's old growth all the way, up the Hot Springs Fork, past Shower Creek and Spray Creek, and eventually into the Bull of the Woods Wilderness. You should go at least as far as Shower Creek (0.3 mile past the springs and just 0.1 mile past a camping area on the right) to enjoy the 50-foot falls and a little wooden platform somebody built underneath it for folks to shower on.

As alcohol is allowed and the police are hours away, Bagby is best avoided on weekend nights, when partiers sometimes take over the place. So unless you too are a beer-swilling yahoo, go on a weekday or early on the weekends. For more information, call the Clackamas Ranger District office at (503) 630-4256.

Barlow Pass

IN BRIEF

There's a great view of Mount Hood at the top, and a one-way car-shuttle option that ends at Timberline Lodge, but this convenient, not-too-tough hike is all about the forest. It goes through some of the finest high-elevation old-growth around.

DIRECTIONS

From Portland on US 26, drive 51 miles east of Interstate 205 and turn north on OR 35, following signs for Hood River. After 2.5 miles on OR 35, turn right onto FS 3531, following signs for Barlow Pass and the Pacific Crest Trail (PCT). The trailhead is 0.2 mile ahead on FS 3531.

DESCRIPTION

There are more spectacular hikes in the Mount Hood area, but none has the combination of solitude and old-growth beauty that this one offers. It's also perfect for a picnic, or just a dose of sunshine, in a high-altitude meadow with Mount Hood looming over you.

From the trailhead, walk across FS 3531 and into the woods on the Pacific Crest Trail (PCT; #2000). Stop to admire the relief map of the PCT in Oregon and contemplate some of the distances on there. People who hike the whole PCT in a year average about 20 miles a day! You'll get in four miles on the PCT today; note that on the USGS

KEY AT-A-GLANCE INFORMATION

Length:
8 miles

Configuration:
Out-and-back

Difficulty:
Moderate

Scenery:
Forest, meadows, view of Mount Hood, and two river canyons

Exposure:
Forest on the way up, open on top

Traffic:
Use is light.

Trail surface:
Packed dirt with some roots

Hiking time:
3.5 hours

Season:
June through October

Access:
Northwest Forest Pass required

Maps:
USGS Mount Hood South; Mount Hood Wilderness; Green Trails #462 (Mount Hood)

Facilities:
None; no water on the hike

Special comments:
Consider doing this hike as a one-way, 6-mile trek with a second car parked at Timberline Lodge.

Timberline Trail

Timberline Lodge

NORTH

5: Barlow Pass

0.5 mile scale

Viewpoint

5,260'

Timberline Trail

White River

To Hood River

Pacific Crest Trial

35

Salmon River

35

To 26

4,157'

P

5

FS 3531

Barlow Rd.

Mount Hood South map, which was created in 1962, this trail is still labeled the Skyline Trail.

Take the left-most fork of the trails before you, walking north on the PCT toward Mount Hood. You'll take a few steps on an old roadway and, after 0.1 mile, walk across OR 35. The trail continues in a small draw on the far side.

The first part of the trail isn't too exciting; in fact, after a half mile you'll walk through a fairly recent clear-cut. But right after that you'll come into a glorious stand of mostly noble fir, with its long, straight, branchless trunks. In early summer the ground will be blanketed with wildflowers. In fall you'll see berries and red-and-orange vine maple. Stay quiet, especially early in the day, and you'll hear birds and possibly see deer or elk. It's just a pleasant place to be, and the trail's altitude gain (less than 300 feet per mile) is entirely manageable.

At the two-mile mark, you'll enter a more diverse forest, with firs and hemlocks mixed together. Then, at 3.5 miles, you'll come to an overlook of the Salmon River Canyon. The Salmon is the only river in the lower 48 states classified as a Wild and Scenic River from its headwaters to its mouth, and here you're looking at its headwaters. It starts right up the hill there at the Timberline Ski Area and winds up down at the Sandy River along US 26. Two hikes along the lower Salmon are the Salmon River Trail and Wildwood Recreation Area; see page 144 for Salmon River and page 198 for Wildwood Recreation Area.

Just after this point, the forest will start to open up, revealing bear grass and meadows filled with August wildflowers. After four miles, you'll intersect the Timberline Trail in just such a meadow. Relax here if you'd like and then turn around, or continue left on the Timberline Trail for a half mile to a spectacular lookout onto the White River Canyon, hundreds of feet deep and on your right.

If you've opted to park a car up at Timberline and are doing a one-way hike, keep going up the Timberline Trail toward the mountain. It's 2 more miles to the lodge—2 miles that climb a little over 700 feet in all, so it's not too much more work. You go first along the edge of the White River Canyon and then through meadows, across the tiny Salmon River, and then into the lodge for a nice hot or cold beverage.

NEARBY ACTIVITIES

Right at the beginning of this hike, you walked across the old Barlow Road, an Oregon Trail alternative to the rapids-filled Columbia River. If you've got some clearance on your vehicle, you can drive it for miles, eventually making your way to the Dalles—though the road improves dramatically a long way before the Dalles. See the sign for various mileages. There are several campgrounds along the way.

Beacon Rock State Park

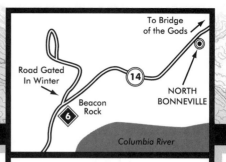

IN BRIEF

One of the most recognized symbols of the Columbia River Gorge, Beacon Rock is also an amazing, if short, hiking experience—and it's not even all this state park has to offer.

DIRECTIONS

From Portland on Interstate 84, drive 37 miles east of Interstate 205 and take Exit 44/Cascade Locks. As soon as you enter the town, take your first right to get on the Bridge of the Gods, following a sign for Stevenson, Washington. Pay a 75-cent toll on the bridge, and at the far end turn left (west) on WA 14. Proceed 6.6 miles to Beacon Rock State Park. To climb Beacon Rock, park on the left; to go toward Hamilton Mountain, turn right on the access road to the campground and drive 0.4 mile to the trailhead.

The gate to the upper trailhead is closed in winter and spring, but the trail is open; you'll just have to park on WA 14 and walk 0.4 mile up the access road.

DESCRIPTION

Beacon Rock got its name—well, its white man's name—on Halloween 1805, when William Clark described it in his journal. For the Corps of Discovery as well as the people who then lived along the Columbia River, Beacon Rock meant two important things: the last of the rapids on the Columbia and the beginning of tidal influence on the river.

KEY AT-A-GLANCE INFORMATION

Length:
1.6 miles to top of Beacon Rock; 7 miles to Hamilton Mountain

Configuration:
Out-and-back

Difficulty:
Moderate (Hamilton Mtn. is hard)

Scenery:
Overlooks of the Columbia River, close-up view of a waterfall

Exposure:
Fairly open

Traffic:
Heavy on weekends

Trail surface:
Packed dirt with rocks, pavement

Hiking time:
1 hour for Beacon Rock, 3.5 hours for Hamilton Mountain

Season:
Year-round. Call for trail conditions.

Access:
No fees or permits needed

Maps:
Green Trails #428 (Bridal Veil)

Facilities:
Water and rest rooms

Special comments:
For more information, phone Columbia River Gorge National Scenic Area at (541) 386-2333.

NORTH

6: Beacon Rock State Park

1 mile scale

Hardy Creek

Hamilton Mtn. 2,438'

Rodney Falls

Viewpoint

Hardy Falls

6

P

14

Road Gated In Winter

6

P

Beacon Rock 848'

Columbia River

Nature Trail

Today, it means a unique hiking experience to its summit, and the state park around it means a chance for more nice views of the Columbia River.

To go up Beacon Rock, start walking at a sign on the south side of WA 14 and get ready to give thanks and admiration to a man named Henry J. Biddle. It was he who bought the rock (which is what's left of the inside of an ancient volcano) specifically to build the trail you're about to hike. That he did so is simply amazing; that he did it with the help of just one other person from October 1915 to April 1918 is almost beyond comprehension.

To get to the top, just keep it up and, if heights bother you, don't look down. It's virtually all rails and bridges and platforms until you're just below the summit, where you'll have a view east to Bonneville Dam, north to Hamilton Mountain, and straight down the other side to the boat docks of the state park. Keep an eye out for rock climbers, and don't throw anything from the top.

For a more challenging and more rewarding hike, drive (or walk, if the gate is closed) up the road across WA 14 to the campground and the Hamilton Mountain trailhead. You'll climb gently through forest until you reach a bench to take a break, although the power lines you're under aren't all that scenic. At half a mile, stay right at a trail junction, and 0.9 mile later you'll come to a sign saying HAMILTON MOUNTAIN and pointing downhill.

For a sight to remember, and also if you'd like a soaking to cool you down go left a couple hundred yards and check out Rodney Falls, which almost explodes out of a bowl in the rock face. You can

get right in its spray, if you don't mind essentially wading throughout the last part of the trail.

If you don't feel like climbing anymore, turn back here, as it gets tougher quickly. For Hamilton Mountain, follow the signed trail as it crosses Hardy Creek and then heads up the hill. After 0.2 mile of climbing, you'll come to a trail junction; to the left is the return portion of a possible loop hike, but keep to the right, and after some sturdy climbing you'll reach a spectacular rock lookout. There's nothing wrong with turning around here, but be careful as you walk around on these rocks—in some spots it's more than 200 feet straight down.

But if you want the real view, keep going up—another 700 feet in just over a mile—until you reach a junction on top of the mountain. The view south is somewhat blocked by brush, but you can see up to Table Mountain (see page 157) to the northeast and Mount St. Helens to the northwest. The scenery is better on the route you just came up, but if you want to complete the loop, continue back along the ridge for 0.9 mile, turn left onto an old road, pick up another trail less than a mile later, and follow that trail through the woods for another mile. That puts you back at the junction mentioned above, just east of Rodney Falls. Turn right and you'll be back at the trailhead in 1.6 miles.

NEARBY ACTIVITIES
The Columbia Gorge Interpretive Center, a few miles west on WA 14 in Stevenson, features historical displays ranging from the geological (formation of the gorge) to the steam engines used on railroads a bit more recently.

Breitenbush

To Detroit

FS 46

FS 46   7   FS 4685

Cleator Bend
Campground   Optional
Parking &
Trailhead at
Hot Springs   7

IN BRIEF

With its combination of old-growth majesty and New Age spirituality, the area around Breitenbush Hot Springs is one of the most peaceful and inspiring places in Oregon. The trails are easy, the surroundings are sublime, and the water is hot.

DIRECTIONS

From Portland on Interstate 5, drive 35 miles south of Interstate 205 and take Exit 253/Stayton/Detroit Lake. Turn left (east) onto OR 22 and follow it 49 miles to Detroit. Turn left onto FS 46. For the roadside trailhead, travel 12.2 miles, turn right onto FS 4685, and go a half mile to the trailhead on the right. For the hot springs from Detroit, go 10 miles on FS 46 and turn right onto a one-lane bridge just past the Cleator Bend Campground. Over the next 1.5 miles, stay left at three junctions and you're there.

DESCRIPTION

Like a bay of tranquility amid a sea of logging operations, the area along the South Fork of the Breitenbush River is often described with words like *peaceful,* *magical,* and *special.* The resort is a draw unto itself—with its pools, tubs, well-being programs, massage, and other healing arts—but the forest and the river beckon for easy, pleasant walks.

One option is to simply go to the hot springs resort, register as a day user (see "Nearby Activities" on p. 30) and start

KEY AT-A-GLANCE INFORMATION

Length:
Recommended hike, 5.2 miles

Configuration:
Out-and-back

Difficulty:
Moderate

Scenery:
Ancient forests and a raging river

Exposure:
Shady all the way

Traffic:
Moderate to light

Trail surface:
Packed dirt with a few roots

Hiking time:
2.5 hours

Season:
Year-round

Access:
Northwest Forest Pass required to park on FS 4685; day-use fee required to park at the hot springs

Maps:
USGS Breitenbush Hot Springs; free maps available at resort office

Facilities:
None at the trailhead; all are available at the hot springs.

Special comments:
A one-way hike with a car shuttle will leave you at the hot springs.

FS 46

FS 4685

P

7

South Breitenbush Trail

Roaring Creek

Breitenbush Gorge

Emerald Forest Trail

Tree Trail

Devils Ridge Trail

South Fork Breitenbush River

P

Parking at Resort

Spotted Owl Trail

Campground

NORTH

0.5 mile scale

7: Breitenbush

your hiking on the Spotted Owl Trail, which starts across from the resort parking lot. After 1.1 miles on that trail, you'll come to a junction with the Tree Trail, which in half a mile joins the Emerald Forest Trail. At that point, you've connected to the loop hike recommended below, which begins on FS 4685.

From the parking area on FS 4685, walk 0.1 mile down the trail and turn left onto the South Breitenbush Gorge National Recreation Trail. You will only hear the river at this point, so for views you'll have to settle for the big Douglas firs, hemlocks, and western red cedars towering over you and the oxalis and early-summer wildflowers below you. Rhododendrons will be blooming here in June.

After 0.7 mile, you'll come to a trail on the right, leading downhill, with a sign saying EMERALD FOREST. Ignore this one for now and keep going. In this area you will see what a big winter storm can do to even these mighty trees. In 1990 a storm blew down many of these trees and closed the trail for a year; another one, on Thanksgiving 1999, took out some bridges over the river. After 0.8 mile, a short side trail will lead down to the Breitenbush Gorge, a 100-yard-long, 40-foot-deep chasm that the river rips through. You can turn around here or go another half a mile on the main trail to a beautiful footbridge over Roaring Creek; this area also has much better views of the river. You might as well explore it, because the total elevation change is practically nothing.

Now make your way back to the first trail, the one you ignored before. Take it now, and go 0.1 mile down the hill to the South Breitenbush Trail, which you'll cross on a bridge. The 1999 storm rolled this one-log bridge over on its side, officially closing it for over a year. But Oregonians, being the folks they are, crossed it anyway; they (myself included) simply walked on the rails and held onto the log. However you get across (the bridge was set to be rebuilt in 2001) you'll climb briefly on the Emerald Forest Trail and then stroll through as pretty a forest as you'll ever see. By the end of the trail, one mile later when you intersect the Tree Trail and the Devils Ridge Trail, you'll be in what is known as a "climax forest." This, in other words, is what a forest looks like after thousands of years of being left alone—no humans, no major fires, no storms to blow everything down. If you put in about 0.1 mile on the Tree Trail, you'll walk between the rootballs of two trees that fell in opposite directions at the same time. You can also explore along the Devils Ridge Trail, which climbs some 900 feet in less than a mile to a lookout.

If you parked a car at the hot springs, keep going on the Tree Trail until it intersects the Spotted Owl Trail, and in 1.1 miles on that one you'll be ready to soak. If, instead, you turn around at the end of the Emerald Forest Trail and go back to your car, that's the 5.2-mile loop.

NEARBY ACTIVITIES

Breitenbush Hot Springs is open from 9 a.m. to 6 p.m. to day-use visitors, but advance reservations are required. You'll have access to the pools, steam room, and daily well-being programs. The cost is on a sliding scale (based on your ability to pay) and ranges from $8 to $15.

Bull of the Woods

IN BRIEF

This is like two great hikes in one: an easy stroll through old-growth forest and rhododendrons to two beautiful lakes, and a more challenging climb to a fire lookout tower with a panoramic view.

DIRECTIONS

From Portland on OR 224, travel 44 miles southeast of Interstate 205, through the town of Estacada, to the ranger station at Ripplebrook. Turn right onto FS 46 and, 3.6 miles later, right again onto FS 63. After 5.7 miles, turn right onto FS 6340, following a sign for Bull of the Woods and Pansy Basin. At a junction 3.5 miles later, stay straight, still on FS 6340. Then, 4.4 miles past that junction (7.9 miles after FS 63), turn right on FS 6341, ignoring a sign to the left saying BULL OF THE WOODS TRAIL. Our trailhead is 3.6 miles ahead on the right.

DESCRIPTION

This trail has it all. Come in June, as soon as the snow has cleared, and let your mind be boggled by the rhododendron show among the old-growth towers on the way to Pansy Lake.

Come in late summer and pick huckleberries up on the ridge. Or come in fall, when the ridge will be awash in color and the mountains might have their first coat of snow. Just make sure you get here.

KEY AT-A-GLANCE INFORMATION

Length:
2.2 miles round-trip to Pansy Lake; 7 miles round-trip to Bull of the Woods

Configuration:
Out-and-back

Difficulty:
Easy to Pansy Lake; moderate to Bull of the Woods

Scenery:
Old-growth forest, a mountain lake; rhododendrons, huckleberries

Exposure:
In the shade to the top of the ridge

Traffic:
Moderate on summer weekends, light otherwise

Trail surface:
Packed dirt with some roots, then a few rocks up top

Hiking time:
1 hour to Pansy Lake, 4 hours for all

Season:
June through October

Access:
Northwest Forest Pass required

Maps:
USGS Bull of the Woods; USFS Bull of the Woods Wilderness

Facilities:
None

Trailhead
3,540'

NORTH

8: Bull of the Woods

0.25 mile scale

Dickey
Lake

Pansy Lake
3,994'

Bull of the Woods
5,523'

The peak is the second-highest point in the 27,000-acre Bull of the Woods Wilderness, which boasts more than a dozen lakes bigger than an acre, 68 miles of hiking trails, and even the world-famous northern spotted owl, which you almost certainly won't see.

From the trailhead, you start right out through a beautiful forest, walking basically flat for 0.8 mile, across some nice little creeks and through gauntlets of

rhododendrons, until you reach a trail junction. To visit Pansy Lake, stay straight here (choosing Trail #549) and go 0.2 mile. There's a campsite to your right on the shoreline that's excellent for picnicking.

To head for Bull of the Woods, go back to the main trail and turn right (uphill); this would be a left turn if you were coming from the trailhead and didn't go to Pansy Lake. After another half a mile of climbing, a faint trail to the right leads 0.1 mile to tiny Dickey Lake. It's worth seeing, but the little trail going off to the left, along its shore, goes nowhere special. If, on the main trail, you get to a small clearing with some rocks on the trail, you missed the trail to Dickey Lake by about 100 yards.

After another 0.8 mile of gradual climbing, you'll reach a trail junction just below the ridge top. Turn right onto Trail #550, the Bull of the Woods Trail, which you skipped back when you were driving to the trailhead. (It has climbed the ridge from your left, but you've come a much more interesting way.) You're now 1.1 miles and about 600 feet in elevation from the summit.

You'll just walk along the ridge, with occasional views out toward Mounts Jefferson and Hood to the left and a nice view down into a noble fir stand to the right.

When you pop out of the forest you'll see the lookout tower to your left. It's one of the few still around, and you can get up on its deck. Jefferson, some 20 miles away, dominates the view from up

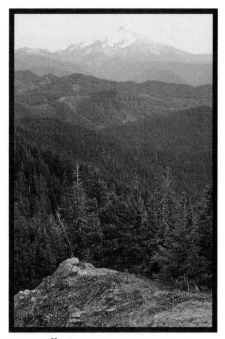

Mount Jefferson
from the lookout on Bull of the Woods

here, but on a clear day you can see all the way from the Three Sisters (right of Jefferson) to Mount Rainier. As the crow flies, it's about 175 miles between the Sisters and Rainier.

Cape Falcon

IN BRIEF

This is one of the best hikes on the Oregon coast. It's easy to get to, it's basically flat, and it offers great views and soothing forest. No wonder it's so popular!

DIRECTIONS

From Portland on US 26, travel 74 miles west of Interstate 405 and turn south on US 101. The trailhead is 14 miles ahead on the right. There are actually three parking areas in succession here. The first (unmarked) one on the right is for Cape Falcon. The second one, 0.1 mile farther on the left, is where the rest room is located. The third is one of the trailheads for Neahkahnie Mountain.

DESCRIPTION

Getting out of your car and onto the Cape Falcon Trail is what hiking on the Oregon coast is all about. You're barely an hour from the Portland metro area, and then after about five steps you're in a rare, coastal, old-growth forest, walking a wide, flat path to a wonderful destination. You'll cruise along for 0.4 mile to a junction. Short Sand Beach will be to your left and down the hill about 0.5 mile; Cape Falcon will be to the right. Straight ahead will be a nice view of Smugglers Cove.

After turning right, you'll cross a small creek and start winding in and out with the contours of the land. Around 1.3 miles, where the trail makes a sharp left

KEY AT-A-GLANCE INFORMATION

Length:
5 miles

Configuration:
Out-and-back

Difficulty:
Easy

Scenery:
Old-growth forest, waterfalls, and several clifftop vistas of the sea

Exposure:
Shady until the last 200 yards

Traffic:
Use is heavy all summer, especially weekends; it's moderate otherwise.

Trail surface:
Packed dirt with some gravel; mud

Hiking time:
2.5 hours

Season:
Year-round

Access:
No fees or permits needed

Maps:
USGS Arch Cape

Facilities:
There are toilets 0.1 mile down the road from the trailhead, but no water. The water on the trail must be treated.

101

P

9

P

P

Cape
Falcon

Short Sand
Beach

Pacific Ocean

Necarney
Creek

To
Hike 35

turn, there's a downed tree on the right that has left a large, disfigured stump. Some more imaginative hiking friends of mine dubbed this stump the Throne of the Forest King. If you assume the throne, you'll see that your kingdom includes a nice little grove of sitka spruce and hemlock.

With that goofiness behind you, proceed another half mile or so. Just before a footbridge over a creek, you'll notice a small, brushy trail to the left. If you take it about 100 feet you'll come to a hidden little waterfall in the creek. If you take it another 100 yards or so, often having to nearly crawl through the brush, you'll find yourself at the top of an even larger falls that goes right down to the ocean. Just be careful of your footing, or you'll wind up in a heap down on the rocks some 50 feet below. Back at the main trail, look for the big burls on the spruce in this area. You'll also get a different view of the first falls you visited on the side trail.

Just after this the trail starts out Cape Falcon itself for the last half mile. You'll get nice views back into Smugglers Cove and up to Neahkahnie Mountain (see page 119), then you'll dip through the trees once more to a junction at the edge of a brushy, largely treeless area. For the end of the cape, turn left, and walk about 0.2 mile through the gauntlet of brush. Out at the end, you'll be 200 feet above the sea, with Falcon Rock out in front of you. (At the end you'll be at the top of an unrailed 200-foot cliff.) There are some nice spots under the trees to spread out for a picnic.

When you head back to the main trail, turn left for a bit and add some more scenery to your day. This is the Oregon Coast Trail, and in the next mile

or so you'll get three more views of the sea.

When the trail starts climbing inland, you might as well turn back, unless the old-growth magic has you in its grips. There are no more ocean views for a while, but there are plenty of big trees and not many people.

NEARBY ACTIVITIES
I feel quite strongly that the best clam chowder in the world is served at the Ecola Seafood Market in Cannon Beach, about 11 miles north of the trailhead on US 101. It's at the corner of 2nd and Spruce.

Also, this hike is right next to the Neahkahnie Mountain Trail, so you could do both in the same day if you're feeling energetic. For more information, call the Oregon State Parks office at (800) 551-6949.

Cape Lookout State Park

Netarts Bay

To Tillamook

Pacific Ocean

3 Capes Scenic Route

10

IN BRIEF

This park offers everything the Oregon Coast is all about: old-growth forest, secluded beaches, clifftop views, and wildlife on land, wing, and water. You've got three options from the trailhead, and with a little energy you could do all three.

DIRECTIONS

From Portland on US 26, drive 20 miles west of Interstate 405, then bear west on OR 6, following a sign for Tillamook. Drive 51 miles to Tillamook, and at the intersection with US 101 stay straight. At that intersection and from then on, you will be following signs for Cape Lookout State Park and the 3 Capes Scenic Route. After crossing US 101, go two blocks and turn left on Stillwell Street. Go two more blocks and turn right onto 3rd Street. Travel 4.9 miles and turn left. After 5.3 miles you'll pass the state park campground and day-use area; this is where you can stash a second car to do the shuttle. The trailhead is 2.7 miles past the campground on the right.

DESCRIPTION

When you park at this trailhead, you will have rare advantages in the world of hiking: multiple options, and it's all downhill from here. Of course, you'll have to come back uphill to get to the car, but even the 800-foot climb from the beach

KEY AT-A-GLANCE INFORMATION

Length:
5 miles round-trip to end of cape; 4 miles round-trip to South Beach; 4.6 miles round-trip to picnic area

Configuration:
All three hikes are out-and-backs.

Difficulty:
All three hikes are moderate.

Scenery:
Old-growth forest, cliffs high above the sea, whales in winter and spring.

Exposure:
Shady, then open at the end

Traffic:
Heavy on summer weekends

Trail surface:
Gravel, packed dirt, mud

Hiking time:
2 hours to the end of the cape; 1.5 hours to South Beach; 2 hours to the picnic area

Season:
Year-round, with mud and possibly storms in winter and spring

Access:
No fees or permits needed

Maps:
USGS Sand Lake

Facilities:
None at the trailhead; rest rooms and water at the campground

10: Cape Lookout State Park

NORTH

0.5 mile scale

Picnic Area

3 Capes Scenic Route

South Beach

Memorial

Viewpoint

Pacific Ocean

Pacific Ocean

South Beach and Cape Lookout

is so well graded you'll hardly be winded when it's done.

Start with the best of the trails, the one out the cape. Take the trail behind the sign at the far end of the lot, and when you get to a junction in 100 yards or so, stay straight. You'll be hiking through that rarest of treats, a coastal, old-growth forest. There are some nice sitka spruces and hemlocks in here, and the whole thing is as peaceful as can be. Just past half a mile out, you'll come to plaque honoring the flight crew of a B-17 bomber that crashed into the cape just west of there in 1943. After another half a mile you'll get a view north; look for the three rocks just off Cape Meares and the town of Oceanside. You can make out an arch in the middle rock; in fact, all three have such arches, and they're called Three Arch Rocks. When you get to some moderately nerve-wracking drop-offs on the left, along with inspiring views south, you're almost done.

At the tip of the cape, you're looking 400 feet straight down at the crashing sea. On a calm day—which is rare in a place that gets 100 inches of rain per year—it's not uncommon to see seals or sea lions down there. But the main attraction is the whales. Thousands of them make the trip each year from the Bering Sea in Alaska to Baja California, a swim of some 6,000 miles. In November and December, when they go south, they tend to be farther out. But in March and April, they're on their way back north with newborn calves, so they go slower and stay closer to shore. At these times of year, bring binoculars (and a raincoat), and you might see dozens of whales in a day.

On your way back to the trailhead, when you reach the junction, turn right (downhill) and follow this trail down to South Beach. Avoid the temptation to take all the various cutoff trails, as they add to erosion. If the 2-mile, 800-foot-drop trail seems a little tedious (like when the beach looks like it's just right there below you but you're walking more sideways than down), just believe that you'll be thankful for this easier grade on your way back up.

There's often another kind of watchable wildlife on South Beach. My surfer friend John informs us that the cape can really clean up a northwest swell, dude, and it's totally worth hauling the board down there when there's tubes coming in. You'll be stoked! You can also hike down the beach, which extends four miles south to Sand Lake, but eventually you'll get into an area where cars are allowed, which sort of takes away from the wilderness feeling.

The last option from the trailhead is located across the lot, going north on the Oregon Coast Trail. It's 2.3 miles, all downhill, to the picnic area and nature trail, down by the campground. You'll pass a couple of viewpoints on the way, including one of Sphinx Island. If you left another car there, your whole day can be a total of 11.3 manageable miles.

If you had only one car, you'll have to come back up to the car at the end of the day, stretching things out to almost 13 miles, so it might not be worth it.

Note: There is a protective cable at the end of the cape, but in other places you'll be right at the top of a 400-foot cliff. If you have two cars, put one down at the campground/picnic area. You'll have to pay a $3 day-use fee there, but at the end of the day you can walk downhill just 2.3 miles from the trailhead back to your second car. There's also a short nature trail there. For more information, call Cape Lookout State Park at (503) 842-4981.

NEARBY ACTIVITIES

As long as you're in Tillamook, take advantage of its tourist stops, most notably the collection of World War II airplanes at the Air Museum south of town and the two cheese factories to the north. The Tillamook Cheese Factory is the best known, but there are slightly more exotic choices at the Blue Heron Cheese Factory.

Cape Meares

IN BRIEF

From a historic lighthouse to a wildlife refuge, Cape Meares is an excellent place to stop and stretch your legs. You can walk a beach, see a couple of massive spruces, and possibly catch a glimpse of elk.

DIRECTIONS

From Portland on US 26, drive 20 miles west of Interstate 405, then bear west on OR 6, following a sign for Tillamook. Drive 51 miles to Tillamook, and at the intersection with US 101 stay straight. At that intersection and from then on, you will be following signs for the 3 Capes Scenic Route and Cape Meares State Park. After crossing US 101, go two blocks and turn left on Stillwell Street. Go two more blocks and turn right onto 3rd Street. Stay on the Scenic Route for 10 miles, then turn right into Cape Meares State Park. The trailhead for the beach loop is immediately on your right. For the lighthouse area, continue down the road 0.6 mile to the parking area.

DESCRIPTION

When you get to Cape Meares, start down in the lighthouse area for a little warm-up. The lighthouse itself is 0.2 mile down from the parking lot, and from May through September it's open for tours. Even if it isn't open, go and check out the views, which are excellent on the

KEY AT-A-GLANCE INFORMATION

Length:
0.6 mile to see the lighthouse and Octopus Tree; 3.5 miles to walk the loop to the beach

Configuration:
Loop

Difficulty:
Easy near lighthouse, moderate to the beach

Scenery:
Panoramas of the sea, trees both large and bizarre, a quiet beach

Exposure:
Shady except on the beach

Traffic:
Heavy around the lighthouse, especially during summer. On the beach loop, use is light.

Trail surface:
Packed dirt, gravel, mud in spots

Hiking time:
0.5 hour around the lighthouse, 2 hours to do the beach loop

Season:
Year-round

Access:
No fees or permits needed

Maps:
USGS Netarts

Facilities:
Toilets at the parking lot; no water

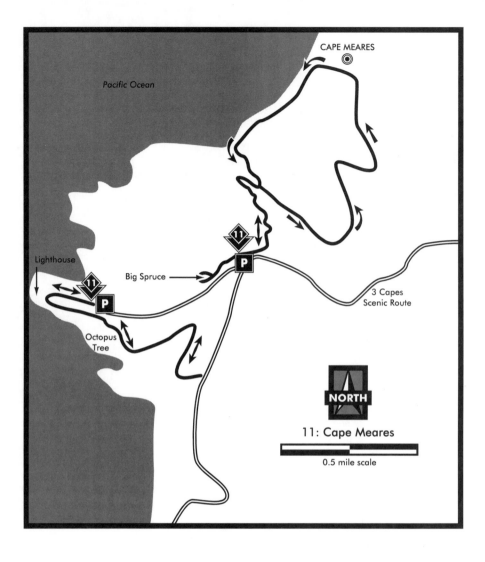

Pacific Ocean

CAPE MEARES

Lighthouse

Big Spruce

3 Capes
Scenic Route

Octopus
Tree

NORTH

11: Cape Meares

0.5 mile scale

way down there and from the lighthouse itself. When you start back up the hill to the parking lot, stay right and follow another trail up the southern side of the point for even more views that way.

Beyond the parking lot going the other way, you'll go 0.1 mile past the rest room to the Octopus Tree, a gnarled, crazy-looking sitka spruce. Its main trunk is 12 feet thick, but the combined width of all the trunks is more like 50

feet. There's another fine view south here, including some houses perched amazingly high on seaside bluffs.

Now that you're warmed up, drive back up the road and park at the upper trailhead. Head into the woods and turn immediately left to witness yet another tree phenomenon. The "Big Spruce," 0.2 mile down the way, isn't so much weird as it's just plain huge—16 feet thick, almost 200 feet tall, and more than 400 years old. The trail goes all the way around it, giving you the full view.

Now head down the hill, switching back and forth among (and sometimes under) old-growth trees. Keep an eye out for a view north to Bayocean Spit, a four-mile sandbar separating Tillamook Bay from the ocean. After 0.7 mile, you'll come to a junction. If you just want to head for the beach, it's 0.2 mile straight ahead. But take the trail right to make a loop. You'll walk 0.8 mile through an area that isn't so fascinating to look at, but it is a National Wildlife Refuge, and there are a fair number of elk who live there. If you would like to see them, you'll need to stay quiet, leash your dog, and be lucky.

This trail ends at a gate in the town of Cape Meares. Cross the gate, take a left on Pacific Avenue, and walk down to the beach. Turn left on the beach. If the tide is low, you'll be able to walk 0.4 mile, and right before you run out of beach you'll notice a trail going up through a grassy notch to your left. Take that for 0.2 mile to a junction, turn right, then keep going up the hill another 0.7 mile back to your car. If the tide is too high, you might not be able to get to the trail from the beach, in which case you'll have to retrace your steps. That wouldn't be so awful, but it does add a little more than a mile to your day.

NEARBY ACTIVITIES

The town of Rockaway (14 miles north of Tillamook on US 101) has a nice beach, plenty of shops, and an old-growth cedar grove owned by the Nature Conservancy.

Cascade Head

IN BRIEF

Imagine standing high atop a windswept, flower-covered prairie, with the sea and the coast spread out below you and not a tree to block the view. Or imagine peeking into a hidden cove where sea lions bark, a waterfall plunges, and waves crash. Well, you don't have to imagine either scene: You can go to Cascade Head and make it happen.

DIRECTIONS

From Downtown Portland on Interstate 5, drive three miles south and take Exit 294/Tigard/Newberg. Bear right onto OR 99 West and follow it 22 miles. Just past the town of McMinnville, turn left onto OR 18 and follow it for 51 miles to its intersection with US 101. Turn right (north) on US 101.

For the lower, year-round trailhead to the Nature Preserve, go one mile north and turn left onto Three Rocks Road. Follow this for two miles, turn left, and park at Knight Park. To reach the trailhead, walk back to the road and turn left for 0.2 mile.

For the two upper trailheads, go 3.8 miles north of OR 18 on US 101 and turn left onto unsigned FS 1861, just before the top of a hill on US 101. Stay left at 2.4 miles, still on FS 1861. The upper Nature Preserve trailhead is 0.8 mile after this turn, on the left. The Harts Cove trailhead is at the end of the road, one mile later.

KEY AT-A-GLANCE INFORMATION

Length:
5.4 miles round-trip to Harts Cove; 2 to 3.4 miles round-trip to the Nature Preserve

Configuration:
Out-and-back

Difficulty:
Moderate, with an easy option

Scenery:
Old-growth forest, waterfalls, sea cliffs, wildflowers, and wildlife

Exposure:
In the forest at first, then open

Traffic:
Use is heavy on summer weekends but moderate otherwise

Trail surface:
Packed dirt with some roots

Hiking time:
3 hours to Harts Cove; 1–1.5 hours for the Nature Preserve

Season:
The upper trailheads are open July 16–December 31. The lower trailheads are open year-round.

Access:
No fees or permits needed

Maps:
USGS Neskowin

Facilities:
No facilities; no water on the trail

NORTH

12: Cascade Head

0.5 mile scale

Chitwood Creek

150'

Harts Cove Viewpoint

Pacific Ocean

Cliff Creek

P

12
970'

FS 1861

P

12
1,300'

Viewpoint
1,217'

Viewpoint
1,217'

Pacific Ocean

12   120'

P

Salmon River

Three Rocks Rd.

Looking south from the Nature Preserve at Cascade Head

DESCRIPTION

First, the Harts Cove Trail. When it starts out, you might think you've got it made, because it's all downhill. It's pretty steep, too—it loses about 500 feet in the first half a mile. Too bad you have to walk back up that at the end of the hike. The forest here is a young one of mostly sitka spruce; notice how only the tops of trees are green? That's because these lower portions don't get any sun, but not because they're unhealthy. Notice, also, the very large stumps around; there's one right on the side of the trail that you can get on top of and measure for yourself.

After 0.7 mile you'll cross Cliff Creek and walk into a different world. Here you can find out what a sitka spruce looks like after about 300 years. You'll also get to hear what hundreds of sea lions sound like—they're to the left, and you might get to see some of them later. Now the hiking gets flatter, as you go out to the end of the ridge to a bench with a view of Harts Cove ahead. Then

you'll wrap back around to the right, through the drainage of Chitwood Creek. Half a mile after the bench, you'll walk under a massive blown-down spruce and then out into the meadows on top of the bluff—yet another world visited on this hike.

It's important to stay on the trails here, as this area is fragile. If you come in August, you'll be wading through a view that looks like it was lifted from the upper reaches of Mount Hood: Look for goldenrod, lupine, Indian paintbrush, and violets. Follow the trail that aims at some trees on the left; there's a wonderful spot to sit down there, and it has a front-row view into Harts Cove. The waterfall you see is that of Chitwood Creek, which you just crossed. As for the sea lions, louder than ever, they are mostly around the point to the south, but if you have binoculars you might be able to see some of them lounging on rocks or the far beach.

There's no real beach access here, but you can get close to the water. From the trees, walk west and stay to the left. There's a steep trail there, almost a slide in spots, that you can take down 0.1 mile to the rocky shore. This rock, and all of Cascade Head in fact, is lava that flowed up through the water. If you make your way to the right 100 yards or so on the rock, you'll have a fabulous view of the headland and north to Cape Kiwanda and, farther off, Cape Lookout.

Now, for the Cascade Head Nature Preserve, you have two options for where to start. If the upper road is open, start up there. The trail, actually an old roadbed, goes flat for one mile through a young and unexciting forest to the main-attraction meadow.

Over 30 years ago this meadow was slated to become a housing development, but conservation-minded folks banded together, bought it, and donated it to the Nature Conservancy. Now also designated as a United Nations Biosphere Reserve, it's protected as the home of the Oregon silverspot butterfly, whose caterpillar will eat only a rare violet that lives in these meadows. That's why FS 1861 and the upper part of the trail is closed from January 1 through July 15.

Once you're out in the meadow, you can go as far as you want. It's 1.7 miles

down (and 1,200 feet of elevation loss) to the lower trailhead; just remember that you will have to walk back up. But you should go as far as a clifftop viewpoint that's just below the tree line in front of you. From there, you can see down to a secluded beach where the surf pounds and sea lions might be lounging.

If you started at the lower trailhead, you'll go through forest for just over a mile before coming out in the meadow. The top of the meadow (where the upper trail comes out of the woods) is 0.6 mile above you.

For more information, contact the Nature Conservancy at (503) 230-1221 or the Hebo Ranger District office at (503) 392-3161.

NEARBY ACTIVITIES
Back on OR 18, a mile before you came to US 101, you went through the town of Otis. You might not have noticed it (it only has about a dozen buildings), but it's the home of an Oregon coast tradition, the Otis Cafe. It's got 28 seats, a line outside, and the biggest portions this side of a logging camp. They're famous for sourdough pancakes and wholewheat molasses toast. If you're interested the whole town of Otis is for sale—for $3 million.

Clackamas River

IN BRIEF

Convenient, not too tough, and not terribly long, the Clackamas River Trail is a perfect way to stretch out your legs and enjoy the scenery among old trees and along a beautiful river.

DIRECTIONS

From Portland on OR 224, travel 33 miles southeast of Interstate 205. Fifteen miles past the town of Estacada, just after crossing two bridges in quick succession, turn right onto Fish Creek Road. Go past the Fish Creek Campground, cross another bridge, and park in the parking lot on the right. The trail starts across the road on your left. To leave a car at the other end, stay on OR 224 for seven more miles and turn right into the Indian Henry Campground. The trailhead is a half a mile up on the right.

DESCRIPTION

It's that rare nice day in winter or early spring—"nice" meaning it's not pouring—and you want to get out and do some hiking. Or it's blazing hot in summer and you want to visit a cool, shady place. Or it's autumn and you want to see the fall colors. Whatever the time, it's always a nice day to go out and hike the Clackamas River Trail. If you can work it out to bring a second car to be stashed at Indian Henry, it'll be that much better. Otherwise, you can do essentially the same distance and make a fine day of it.

KEY AT-A-GLANCE INFORMATION

Length:
7.8 miles one-way with a car shuttle or 7.2 miles round-trip to Pup Creek Falls

Configuration:
Point-to-point or out-and-back

Difficulty:
Moderate

Scenery:
Old-growth forest, a white-water river, and a few waterfalls

Exposure:
Shady all the way

Traffic:
Use is heavy on summer weekends but light to moderate otherwise

Trail surface:
Packed dirt with roots and rocks

Hiking time:
3 hours for either option

Season:
Year-round; muddy in winter and spring

Access:
Northwest Forest Pass required

Maps:
Green Trails #492 (Fish Creek Mountain)

Facilities:
Toilets at the trailhead. The water along the way must be treated.

Clackamas
River

224

P

13

Dog
Creek

Campground

Fish
Creek

Pup
Creek
Falls

The
Narrows

Viewpoint

Pup
Creek

NORTH

Cat
Creek

13: Clackamas River

1 mile scale

Indian Henry
Campground

P

224

Clackamas
River

From the trailhead, you'll start out in a flat section with the river a short distance to your left. After a half mile you'll come to a river access point with moss-covered rocks and a sandy beach—perfect for chilling out or, if you've got small kids, perhaps for turning around. Soon after, you'll come into the first exceptional old-growth forest, with five-foot-thick Douglas firs and even bigger western red cedars. In the next mile or

so of trail, you'll do a little climbing and occasionally find yourself with some pretty serious drops to and views of the river to your left.

If you're wondering about a good place to picnic, you'll find it 2.5 miles up in a campground. There's a stupendous western red cedar right by the water here and plenty of places to sit and contemplate the river. Highway 224 is right across the river, by the way, but you'll rarely notice it. Again, if you've got kids, think about turning around here, because during the next mile you'll go up, down, then up again (a couple hundred feet each time) and occasionally find the river some 200 feet far below you.

After a total of 3.5 miles, after you've dropped down the hill and found yourself under power lines, you'll come to Pup Creek, which the main trail crosses on a series of stepping stones. A side trail leads 0.1 mile up the creek to a view of beautiful Pup Creek Falls. If you didn't stash a car at Indian Henry, turn around here, and you'll have a 7.2-mile hike. If you did leave the second car there, keep on truckin'.

In 0.9 mile a side trail will lead left to another beach—last chance to get to the river on this hike. Right after that you'll climb to a view up the Clackamas that includes The Narrows, a narrow gouge in ancient lava. Down the other side of this hill, another side trail left will lead 0.1 mile to The Narrows themselves.

By the way, if you've seen some cables crossing the river in a few spots and wondered what that's about, they were put in by Portland General Electric for cable-car access across the river to maintain their power lines.

In the last three miles to Indian Henry Campground you'll cross several side creeks (the biggest one named Cat Creek, a nice complement to Pup Creek), see numerous big cedars, get sprayed by a waterfall, and go under a cliff. About half a mile before the end, keep an eye out for a large stump on the left with a cable wrapped around it leading to another large stump. The Forest Service does that to keep big stumps from rolling down into the river and squashing fishermen or boaters.

As of 1999 mountain bikes were no longer allowed on this trail. For more information, contact the Clackamas Ranger District office at (503) 630-4256.

NEARBY ACTIVITIES

If it is one of those winter or spring days where the best you can say is "It ain't raining," or if the rain moves in and changes your mind about hiking, stop in Estacada at the Cada Corner coffee shop, where they have fresh-made cookies and a host of board games to play. It's in a little strip mall at the western end of town, right next to Hitching Post Pizza.

Cooper Spur

IN BRIEF

Though it's far from the toughest, this is the highest hiking trail in Oregon—right up into the realm of the mountain climber. You'll be in the world of rock and snow, and you won't even wear yourself out getting there—well, not completely. You'll also get to see the oldest buildings on Mount Hood and the results of a massive landslide.

DIRECTIONS

From Portland on US 26, drive 51 miles east of Interstate 205 and turn north on OR 35, following signs for Hood River. After 17 miles on OR 35, turn left at a sign for Cooper Spur Ski Area. After 2.4 miles, turn left, again following a sign for Cooper Spur Ski Area. In 1.4 miles, stay straight and leave the pavement. Go 8.3 winding miles to a T junction and turn right. The trailhead is half a mile ahead on the right, in the Cloud Cap Saddle campground.

DESCRIPTION

If you want to get way, way up there, this is your hike. In the days before Timberline Lodge and the road to it were built, Cooper Spur was the standard climbing route to Mount Hood's 11,239-foot summit, and people still climb it that way today.

The whole area, in fact, is historically significant. Just up a hill from the trailhead, and at the end of the road, is the Cloud Cap Inn, built in 1889 by two

KEY AT-A-GLANCE INFORMATION

Length:
8.2 miles

Configuration:
Balloon

Difficulty:
Hard

Scenery:
Old-growth forest, glaciers, the upper reaches of Mount Hood

Exposure:
Shady to sunny; plenty of wind, too

Traffic:
Use is moderate on summer weekends but light otherwise.

Trail surface:
Packed dirt, roots, sand, rocks

Hiking time:
4.5 hours

Season:
July to mid-October

Access:
Northwest Forest Pass required

Maps:
USGS Mount Hood North; USFS Mount Hood Wilderness; Green Trails #462 (Mount Hood)

Facilities:
Outhouse and water at the trailhead

Special comments:
Bring warm clothing. Weather at this altitude can change quickly.

Cloud Cap Inn

FS 3512

P

14

5,860'

Tilly Jane
Historic Area

Viewpoint

Timberline
Trail

Tilly Jane
Loop

6,640'

Timberline
Trail

Eliot Glacier

NORTH

14: Cooper Spur

0.5 mile scale

Tie-In
Rock

Cooper Spur
8,514'

prominent Portland families as a recreation destination. It's the oldest building on Mount Hood. The hotel venture never took off, and by World War II the property was given to the Forest Service. In 1956 the Crag Rats, a Hood River–based climbing and rescue organization, took it over, and they maintain it to this day. Although the public can't officially go in, if you're nice to some folks you see there they might let you stick your head in for a bit.

More history later; now, for the hiking. The trail starts at the far end of the camp-ground. Take the Timberline Trail (#600) to the left and enter a rare, snow-zone, old-growth forest, where mountain hemlock and Pacific silver firs get bigger than you'd think in an area that usually has ten feet of snow by the end of November. In 1.2 miles you'll come to a junction just above the forest; following a sign for Cooper Spur, turn uphill—and get used to the climbing.

Just a couple hundred yards up, back among the twisted white bark pines on your right, sits the Cooper Spur shelter at the end of a small side trail. But for our purposes, keep going up. The trail will switch back and forth through the sand and rocks on a manageable grade, and slowly the Eliot Glacier will start to fill your view to the right. You'll hear it pop and rumble as it carves the side of the mountain, and if you're lucky, especially in late summer, you'll see big pieces of it calving and tumbling downhill.

After 2.3 miles of this climbing you'll come to the top of the ridge, where you should look for a rock with some impressive carvings and the date July 17, 1910. It commemorates a Japanese climbing party. Since you've climbed all the altitude at this point, you might as well go another 0.3 mile along the ridge top—just beware that this ridge is thin, rocky, and usually wind-swept.

Just before the snow line, you'll come to a plaque attached to the side of what they call Tie-In Rock; it's called that because it's here that climbers tie themselves to one another to venture out onto the glacier. *Do not* under any circumstances (short of having ropes and crampons and relevant experience) go out onto the glacier. Be satisfied with being at the top of Oregon's hiking world, and sit back among the sheltering rocks to take in the view.

From left to right, with Mount Hood behind you, we have the Eliot Glacier, way off in the distance the bare face of Table Mountain in the Columbia River Gorge, Mount St. Helens, Mount Rainier, Mount Adams, Elk Meadows and Gnarl Ridge down at your feet, Lookout Mountain on a ridge to the east, and then a building below you on a Mount Hood ridge, which is the top of a ski lift at Mount Hood Meadows Ski Area. Now do you feel like you're way up there?

Now look up at Mount Hood. The Cooper Spur climbing route begins on the snowfield right in front of you and proceeds up through the rocks above, tending slightly to your left. As climbers like to say, it's not as steep as it looks. Look for a prominent rock called The Chimney just below the summit and Pulpit Rock more to your right. The rocky area just below the right face of the summit is known as the Chisolm Trail because several members of a Chisolm family fell down it to their deaths. In fact, the Crag Rats say that whenever somebody falls on the Cooper Spur climbing route, they generally wind up within about 200 feet of the same spot at the top of the Eliot Glacier.

On your way down, when you get back to the junction where you originally turned right, stay straight now, leaving the Timberline Trail for the Tilly Jane Loop. After 0.6 mile, you'll come to an overlook of a large, bare bowl on your right. That's what was left behind by the Polallie Slide, a massive debris flow and flood in December 1980 that wiped out parts of OR 35.

A short while later you'll find yourself looking at some old buildings. This is part of the 1,400-acre Tilly Jane Historic Area. This area, by the way, is immensely popular with cross-country skiers, who come up a 2.7-mile trail from Cooper Spur Ski Area and spend the night in some of these buildings. And if you're wondering about that name, Tilly Jane was the nickname of the matriarch of the Ladd family, one of the builders of Cloud Cap Inn.

Now, to get back to your car, just put Mount Hood on your left and follow the trail half a mile back to the trailhead.

Dog Mountain

Wind Mtn. Dog Mtn.

14 15

Columbia River

IN BRIEF

This is probably the most popular of the real hiking trails in the Columbia River Gorge—"real" meaning it requires some real effort. But with an easy-access trailhead, great views of the river, and sunshine and wildflowers at a time when it's still raining in Portland, it's no wonder everybody on earth comes here.

DIRECTIONS

From Portland on Interstate 84, drive 37 miles east of Interstate 205 and take Exit 44/Cascade Locks. As soon as you enter the town, take your first right to get on the Bridge of the Gods, following a sign for Stevenson, Washington. Pay a 75-cent toll on the bridge, and at the far end turn right onto WA 14. Proceed 12 miles to the trailhead on the left. Start early in the day on this one, if only to make sure you get a parking place.

DESCRIPTION

It seems that everyone around Portland who hikes has been up Dog Mountain. Climbers use it as an early-season conditioner. Wildflower enthusiasts flock to it in early summer. In spring, when it's still raining in Portland, it tends to be sunny here. But most people take the main Dog Mountain Trail, which is therefore crowded, and which was also designed, it seems, to punish the legs and lungs of those who would hike it. This thing is steep! You can come down this way, if

KEY AT-A-GLANCE INFORMATION

Length:
6.9 miles

Configuration:
Loop

Difficulty:
Hard

Scenery:
Second-growth forest, wildflowers, and a panoramic view of the Columbia River Gorge

Exposure:
Alternates between shady and open

Traffic:
Use is very heavy on weekends but moderate otherwise.

Trail surface:
Packed dirt with rocks, some gravel

Hiking time:
4 hours

Season:
Year-round, but it occasionally gets snowfall on top.

Access:
Northwest Forest Pass required

Maps:
Trails of the Columbia Gorge; Green Trails #430 (Hood River)

Facilities:
Toilets at the trailhead, but no water

Dog Mtn.
2,948'

Augsberger
Mtn. Trail

Puppy Point
2,505'

14

80' P

15   15

Columbia River

you want, but it's no bargain then, either. Instead, from the parking lot, take the trail on the left, the Augsperger Mountain Trail. It's 0.6 mile longer, but whoever designed it had a much better grasp of the concept of "grade." That's not to say it's easy—it's 3.7 uphill miles, gaining 2,700 feet in elevation. But it's steady, whereas parts of the other trail are insane. So take this one as it contours left, with ever-improving views of the river and Wind Mountain. When you turn right and away from the river, you

will have gone 0.9 mile and gained 400 feet. Not so bad, right? In the next 1.3 miles you'll gain 1,200 feet. That's when the switchbacks start and it gets steep—just remember, this is the "easier" way. The next half a mile gains some 700 feet. Then you'll turn right at a junction.

I'd like to take this moment to explain why Dog Mountain is called Dog Mountain. It's not because of all the dogs on the trail, nor is it because the climb is, well, like a female dog. It's because some pioneers in the area were forced to eat their dogs to avoid starvation. The town of Hood River, Oregon, was in fact first called Dog River, but the name was changed because nobody liked it.

With this knowledge in your head, enjoy a few minutes of flat trail before you climb again and pop out into the sun. Now it's time to claim your reward for all that climbing. In May and June, the open slopes of Dog Mountain are awash in flowers, especially big yellow balsamroot; but year-round, the views here of the river and other mountains—including Mount Hood, which peeks its head over the far side—are sublime. Stroll through this area and know that virtually all your climbing is done. You'll intersect the Dog Mountain Trail after 0.9 mile; turn left and, just 0.1 mile up, you'll be at the top of a sloped meadow with everybody and their dogs.

The view here stretches from the high desert of eastern Oregon to Beacon Rock in the west—look how small it is! Way to the right is Mount St. Helens. Directly across the way is 4,960-foot Mount Defiance, the one with radio towers on top—look how big it is! The highest point in the gorge, it seems to

taunt, "Yeah right, you've climbed barely half of me."

To hike down Dog Mountain, take the scenic loop. From the summit, go left on a trail that soon ducks into the trees, some of which are surprisingly large. Keep an eye out for Mount Adams to the north. This trail rejoins the other branch of the Dog Mountain Trail at a lookout that's actually called Puppy Point (2,505 feet in elevation). Then the bottom drops out, and you lose 600 feet in the next half mile before a junction. You'll save 0.2 mile by going right, but it's worth it to go left for one last view of the river 0.6 mile down. Stay left at another junction 1 mile later, and after a final 0.5 mile you can finally rest your throbbing feet.

For more information, contact the Columbia River Gorge National Scenic Area office at (541) 386-2333.

NEARBY ACTIVITIES

When you get back across to Cascade Locks, take a ride on the Sternwheeler Columbia Gorge, which has several scenic trips per day from mid-June through September.

Eagle Creek

Columbia River

84 To Cascade Locks

Suspension Bridge

Exit 41 (Eagle Creek)

16 Eagle Creek

IN BRIEF

One of the classic and most popular hikes in Oregon, Eagle Creek is the one hike that just about everybody has done part of. That's because it's easy to get to, easy to hike, and several kinds of beautiful. So start early, or go on a weekday, so you won't have to share it with everybody in the state.

DIRECTIONS

From Portland on Interstate 84, drive 34 miles east of Interstate 205 and take Exit 41/Eagle Creek. Go 0.2 mile and turn right, then 0.6 mile to the end of the road. If it's crowded, you might have to park closer to the highway and hike that much farther.

DESCRIPTION

The magic of this hike, at certain times of the year, begins before you even hit the trail itself. Eagle Creek has a small run of fall Chinook salmon—fish that spend their adult lives in the ocean, come more than 70 miles up the Columbia, swim through the fish ladder at Bonneville Dam, and then come here to spawn. A small dam blocks their further progress up Eagle Creek, but in October and November they spawn in little round pools cleared by volunteers to simulate conditions in a wild mountain stream.

The trail was built before 1920 to coincide with the opening of the Columbia River Highway. Although that historic

KEY AT-A-GLANCE INFORMATION

Length:
4.2 miles round-trip to Punchbowl Falls; 13 miles round-trip to Tunnel Falls

Configuration:
Out-and-back

Difficulty:
Moderate

Scenery:
Waterfalls, old-growth forest, spawning salmon in the fall

Exposure:
Mostly shady

Traffic:
Use is heavy throughout the summer but moderate in the spring and fall.

Trail surface:
Packed dirt and rocks

Hiking time:
2 hours to Punchbowl Falls; 5.5 hours to Tunnel Falls

Season:
Year-round, but it will be muddy in the winter and spring.

Access:
Northwest Forest Pass required

Maps:
Trails of the Columbia Gorge

Facilities:
Toilets at the trailhead, but no water

Columbia
River

84

P

Exit 41
Eagle Creek

P

16

Metlako
Falls

Punchbowl
Falls

Loowit
Falls

High Bridge

Skooknichuck
Falls

4.5 Mile
Bridge

NORTH

16: Eagle Creek

1 mile scale

Opal
Creek

Tunnel
Falls

East
Fork

roadway has mostly been gobbled up by Interstate 84, the section from Multnomah Falls to Cascade Locks (which goes right by Eagle Creek) has been converted into a hiking and biking trail, as have a few other sections.

The work that went into the Eagle Creek Trail is really something; they chipped the trail into cliff faces, built High Bridge over the gorge, and put a tunnel behind a falls six miles up. It's work like this that inspired the dedication of this book.

At just under a mile, you'll come to the first place where you walk a ledge with a cable to hang on to. If it's a summer weekend, things can get interesting here while you're trying to negotiate for cable space with dozens of other hikers. At 1.5 miles, you'll come to a viewpoint of Metlako Falls, the first of many such sights of your day. Just past the viewpoint is a bench for resting. At 1.8 miles and another bench, a side trail leads down to Punchbowl Falls, a must-see trip and the end of the line for a lot of people.

Go 0.2 mile down this trail to an unnamed falls; just above that is a large clearing that's often filled with people swimming and sunbathing. At the upstream end of the clearing is a lovely (and often photographed) view of Punchbowl Falls.

If you turn back here, you will have done 4.2 miles, but it's not much more work to go at least as far as High Bridge, another 1.2 miles up. If you head up, in 0.3 mile you'll get a bird's-eye view of Punchbowl Falls; then the gorge narrows considerably. You'll see Loowit Falls on the right just before High Bridge; if you turn around at the bridge, you'll have a seven-mile day. But even if you are turning back, put in another 0.3 mile to a great picnic spot on the left and, 100 yards later, a rare chance for access to the creek itself, in this case at the top of Skooknichuck Falls. Just past that are some very impressive Douglas firs right on the trail.

Continuing up the trail, you'll soon cross what is officially known as Four-and-a-Half Mile Bridge. Now, even the map acknowledges that this is exactly four miles from the trailhead, so what gives? Well, the fish hatchery back at the trailhead wasn't there when the trail was built (there was no need for it, because Bonneville Dam didn't exist yet), so the trailhead used to extend half a mile farther north, to the edge of the Columbia River Highway.

Just past the bridge, look on the right for a double waterfall; that's Opal Creek, but it shouldn't be confused with the world-famous Opal Creek described elsewhere in this book (see page 128). About half a mile above that, a sign explains that the area you're now entering was burned in a 1902 fire; there are still some charred stumps around, in fact. So all the trees you'll see for a while are less than 100 years old.

After 1.5 more miles, bringing your total to 6, you'll come into a deep gorge where Tunnel Falls plunges 130 feet and the trail goes behind it through a 35-foot tunnel. Tunnel Falls is actually on East Fork Creek; to return to Eagle Creek and see one final, dramatic falls, go about 0.2 mile farther. This falls doesn't have a name, but it does have a neat crisscross feature in its upper section. Perhaps it should be called Crisscross Falls.

You can keep going if you want, but if you head back at this point you'll wind up putting in 13 miles. That should be enough for a day, and besides, you get to see everything again on your way back.

For more information, contact the Columbia River Gorge National Scenic Area office at (541) 386-2333.

NEARBY ACTIVITIES

If you didn't get to see fish in Eagle Creek, stop at the fish hatchery at Bonneville Dam on the way home. They have a trout pond with some real lunkers, a sturgeon viewing area with a six-footer swimming around in it, and a fish ladder where at certain times of the year you can see salmon and steelhead swimming up past the dam to spawn. It's one mile west on Interstate 84, and there's no charge for admission.

Elk Meadows

IN BRIEF

Easily one of the most spectacular sights in the Mount Hood area, sprawling and flower-filled Elk Meadows is also relatively easy to get to. Beyond that, several side trips in the area invite you to soaring viewpoints.

DIRECTIONS

From Portland on US 26, drive 51 miles east of Interstate 205 and turn north on OR 35, following signs for Hood River. After seven miles on OR 35, turn left at the second entrance for the Mount Hood Meadows Ski Area (the one for the Nordic Center). The trailhead is half a mile ahead on the right.

DESCRIPTION

If all you're doing is going to Elk Meadows, there's only one hill between you and your destination. But while you're at it, there are some other options worth checking out.

From the trailhead, you'll follow a flat trail through moss-draped forest, pocket meadows with wildflowers, and huckleberries that are ripe in late August. Ignore two trails on the left, the first #667 to Umbrella Falls and the second #646 up Newton Creek. After half a mile you'll cross Clark Creek on a bridge, and after another half a mile you'll cross Newton Creek on logs. This last one might be tricky for small children.

KEY AT-A-GLANCE INFORMATION

Length:
4.5 miles round-trip to Elk Meadows; 11 miles to see it all

Configuration:
Out-and-back with optional loops

Difficulty:
Moderate to Elk Meadows; hard to Gnarl Ridge

Scenery:
Meadows, mountain streams, close-up views of Mount Hood

Exposure:
Shady most of the way

Traffic:
Moderate use on weekends, light otherwise

Trail surface:
Packed dirt with some roots

Hiking time:
2.5 hours to Elk Meadows; 6 hours to see everything

Season:
July to October

Access:
Northwest Forest Pass required

Maps:
Mount Hood Wilderness; Green Trails #462 (Mount Hood)

Facilities:
Outhouse at the trailhead. The water on the trail must be treated.

Viewpoints

Timberline
Trail

Cold
Spring
Creek

Gnarl
Ridge
Trail

Perimeter
Trail

Bluegrass
Ridge Trail

Timberline
Trail

Newton
Creek

Newton
Trail

Clark
Creek

Elk Meadows
5,100'

Elk Mtn.
Trail

Elk Mtn.
5,608'

Viewpoint

To
Umbrella Falls

Elk
Meadows
Trail

Mt. Hood
Meadows
Nordic Area

P   17   4,477'

To
Hood River

35

To 26

Now you are at the hill. In 0.6 mile you'll gain almost 700 feet in a series of long switchbacks—consider it your price of admission to Elk Meadows. Just over the top, you'll come to a four-way intersection. For Elk Meadows, go straight and you'll be there in about three minutes. For a side trip to Elk Mountain, turn right.

The trail to Elk Mountain is not spectacular in and of itself, but it's quiet and woodsy and leads to a nice view east,

across OR 35, to Mount Jefferson to the south. Also, while staying quiet on an August morning hike, I briefly saw two elk up there, bounding through the forest away from me. To get to the lookout, go up 0.6 mile and stay straight at the junction with the Bluegrass Ridge Trail (#647). The lookout is 0.3 mile straight ahead. When you come back, take the Bluegrass Ridge Trail (it would now be a right turn) and follow it half a mile along the ridge top before turning left,

Elk Meadows with Mount Hood in the distance

at a large stone cairn, and plunging 0.4 mile down the Bluegrass Tie Trail (#647B) to Elk Meadows.

Elk Meadows is just about unbelievable. It's basically a circular area of meadows about half a mile in diameter, with islands of trees throughout and streams crisscrossing it. For the good of the flowers and grass, resist the temptation to go meadow-stomping, but by all means find a log or rock on the perimeter and have a sit-down. To complete a loop around the meadows or to explore the other loop available on this hike, turn right when you get to the meadows (regardless of whether you went to Elk Mountain or not).

When you come to a sign for Polallie Campground, stay left on the perimeter trail, and about 30 steps later you'll come to an unmarked trail leading left. That's the trail out into the middle of the meadows, where a stone shelter hosts backpackers most summer nights. It's worth a side trip, if only to be surrounded by the meadows.

Continuing on the perimeter trail, you'll cross Cold Spring Creek, and in about half a mile you'll come to a junction with the Gnarl Ridge Trail (#652). To go back to your car, turn left here, finish the loop around the meadows, and then turn right at the junction with the Elk Meadows Trail. But to go a little higher up toward Mount Hood, stay straight here on the Gnarl Ridge Trail.

After just less than a mile of gradual climbing, you'll come to a trail on the left; ignore it. Just past that you'll get to the Timberline Trail (#600). Here, you can turn right and climb 800 feet in 1.5 miles to a fantastic viewpoint atop Gnarl Ridge; or, you can turn left, stay at the same level, and make a loop back to the car. This way will take you along the west side of Gnarl Ridge (6,540 feet elevation) to a bridgeless crossing of Newton Creek. You can even explore up the creek a ways by walking through the boulder field to your right; just be careful, as even the largest of the rocks can roll when you step on them.

To get back to the car, cross the creek, climb about a quarter of a mile, then turn left at the ridge top onto the Newton Trail (#646). Two miles down that heavily huckleberried trail, you'll intersect with the trail you started all this wandering on, the Elk Meadows Trail; turn right and you'll be back at the trailhead in just over a mile.

For more information, contact the Mount Hood Visitor Information Center at (503) 622-7674.

NEARBY ACTIVITIES

For a little piece of Oregon history, pay your respects at the Pioneer Woman's Grave, off of OR 35 just north of its intersection with US 26. Workers building the old Mount Hood Loop Highway found the woman buried beneath a crude marker; her remains have since been moved twice, and to this day people lay crosses or flowers on the pile of rocks marking her grave.

Forest Park

St. Johns Bridge

Willamette River

18 Germantown Rd.

Bridge Way

IN BRIEF

Thanks to some very forward-thinking people of a century ago, assisted by the forces of nature and economics, Portland now has 4,900 acres of trees, creeks, and canyons within its city limits—something no other American city can claim. The heart of Forest Park is the Wildwood Trail, with numerous access points and loops available all along its length.

DIRECTIONS

For the southern end of the Wildwood Trail, which is in Washington Park, the directions are the same as the Washington Park/Hoyt Arboretum hike. For the northern end of the trail, from Portland on US 30, drive six miles west of Interstate 405 and turn left onto Germantown Road. Go 1.5 miles and park in the lot on the left.

DESCRIPTION

In 1903 a report to the city of Portland recommended setting aside the wooded hillside on the west side of Portland for a forest reserve. It was quite a vision for its time, especially considering the fact that to Oregonians then, deep forests were everywhere—and were a bother. Such things, they reasoned, needed to be destroyed for humans to prosper. But this report (and others in the decades that followed) realized that future generations wouldn't have so many of these big trees and uninhabited areas to contemplate,

KEY AT-A-GLANCE INFORMATION

Length:
28 miles one way—or loop hikes of any distance you wish

Configuration:
Out-and-back or loop

Difficulty:
Easy

Scenery:
Mature forest, deep ravines, quiet creeks, views of far-away volcanoes

Exposure:
Shady

Traffic:
Heavy in the southern part of the park on weekends, otherwise light to moderate

Trail surface:
Packed dirt, rocks, roots

Hiking time:
From 1 hour to 1 year

Season:
Year-round

Access:
No fees or permits needed

Maps:
A free Forest Park map can be obtained at Portland Parks and Recreation (1120 SW 5th Avenue).

Facilities:
Water and toilets available at points throughout the park

Wildwood Trail

St. Helens Rd.

Germantown Rd.

18

P

Willalatin Trail

Willamette River

Gate

Springville Rd.

P

Hardesty Trail

Firelane 7

Wildwood Trail

Leif Ericson Dr.
(No Cars)

Saltzman Rd.

Saltzman Rd.

Gate

Maple Trail

Firelane 1

Chestnut Trail

Leif Ericson Dr.
(No Cars)

Wildwood Trail

Alder Trail

St. Helens Rd.

NORTH

Wildwood Trail

18: Forest Park

Dogwood Trail

1 mile scale

Gate

Thurman St.

Wild Cherry Trail

Stone House

N.W. 28th

Macleay Trail

and they (we) would appreciate a chance to do so. They certainly were correct.

But what's now Forest Park almost got swallowed up by the growing Portland in the early twentieth century. Leif Ericson Drive was put in as part of a residential development plan in 1915, and a logging camp was set up to give work to the unemployed. But, thanks in part to the naturally occurring mudslides of the area, money became a problem. When the city started taxing the vacant lots to pay the bills, many of them went into foreclosure. Then came the Great Depression and World War II; it was only after these interruptions that the original idea of a forest park was resurrected. The city dedicated Forest Park in 1948, and then more or less left it alone, installing few (if any) plans or buildings or designs. Today it is an ever-expanding wild area of almost 5,000 acres, home to more than 100 species of birds and 60 species of mammals, including elk and black bear, who roam in on occasion through a wilderness corridor that connects the area to the Coast Range.

There are 60 miles of hiking trails in Forest Park, virtually all of them connected by the 28-mile-long Wildwood Trail and/or Leif Ericson Drive, a wide, multi-use path that runs for 11 miles parallel to the Wildwood Trail.

What follows is a brief description of the Wildwood Trail, but as you can see on the maps, loop options abound. Several things are helpful about the Wildwood Trail: It's very well marked, it's accessible by car at several points, and throughout its length it is marked by mileposts every quarter mile.

The first few miles of the Wildwood Trail are covered as part of the Washington Park/Hoyt Arboretum hike. Just north of that, Wildwood connects to the Pittock Mansion, at the top of our Macleay Trail hike. After that, around Milepost 5, it drops down to the Audubon Society (also on the Macleay Trail), which can be reached by car as well. North of that, Wildwood crosses Balch Creek Canyon into an area thick with alder and maple.

Just past Milepost 9, Wildwood crosses NW 53rd Street, where car access is available. At Milepost 11 there's a large meadow. North of there, the forest turns to older cedars and firs, where woodpeckers roam and sign of deer and coyote may be found. At Milepost 16, the trail crosses NW Saltzman Road—again, car access is available here, though the trail is one mile up the road from a locked gate.

Now you're in a seldom-visited section of the park—an area where native trees and plants dominate. In many other areas of the park, introduced species— especially English ivy, which creates "ivy deserts," where nothing else grows— have taken over. At Milepost 18, you'll get a view of Mount Hood. At Milepost 19 you'll get views of Swan Island and the University of Portland, across the Willamette River. Starting around Milepost 22, you'll start a long descent— through fantastic old-growth fir, hemlock, and cedar—until you reach NW Germantown Road, just past Milepost 24. That's where the northern trailhead parking, described above, is located.

There's still more to the Wildwood Trail, however, and in some ways what lies north of NW Germantown Road is the most spectacular part of Forest Park. This is the least-visited part of the park, and therefore it is the most inhabited by wildlife. From the parking area on Germantown Road, you can go south and explore some of the loops available, or go north for a 7.4-mile out-and-back to NW Skyline Boulevard at the northern terminus of the Wildwood Trail.

Historic Columbia River Highway

IN BRIEF

When it was completed in 1922, the Columbia River Highway was an engineering marvel, known as the "King of Roads." Now it's a historic relic. Some of it can still be driven, but more than ten miles of it have now been restored for hiking and biking only. It's an interesting way to see the Columbia River Gorge, and the Mosier Twin Tunnels (less than a mile from a trailhead in Mosier) are well worth a visit on their own.

DIRECTIONS

All the trailheads lie east of Portland on Interstate 84. *For the eastern section:* Park at either Hood River or Mosier. For Hood River, take Exit 64, make two quick rights (the first right is unnamed; the second right is OR 35), and proceed 0.1 mile to the four-way stop. Turn left onto US 30 and travel 1.4 miles to the parking area. For Mosier, take Exit 69, turn right at the stop sign, then left in 0.1 mile. The trailhead is 0.8 mile ahead on the right, but parking is 0.1 mile beyond it on the left. *For the middle section:* Park at either Starvation Creek State Park (Exit 55) or Viento State Park (Exit 56, then turn right). *For the western section:* Park at either Bonneville Dam or Cascade Locks. To park near Bonneville Dam, take Exit 40. If you're headed west to Moffett Creek, the parking lot is just ahead on the right; if you're headed east to Eagle Creek and Cascade Locks, the

KEY AT-A-GLANCE INFORMATION

Length:
Moffett Creek to Cascade Locks is 6 miles one-way. Hood River to Mosier is 4.6 miles one-way.

Configuration:
Point-to-point or out-and-back

Difficulty:
Easy

Scenery:
Overlooks of the Columbia River

Exposure:
Mostly shady

Traffic:
Varies by section, heavy to light

Trail surface:
Paved

Hiking time:
Moffett to Eagle Creek, 2.5 hours; Hood River to Mosier, 2 hours

Season:
Year-round

Access:
$3 fee to park in Hood River or Mosier; Northwest Forest Pass required at Cascade Locks and Eagle Creek

Maps:
Available at Hood River trailhead

Facilities:
The Hood River trailhead has rest rooms and water.

19: Historic Columbia River Highway

NORTH

0.25 Mile Scale

Columbia River

Eighteenmile Island

To Mosier

Viewpoint

To Hood River

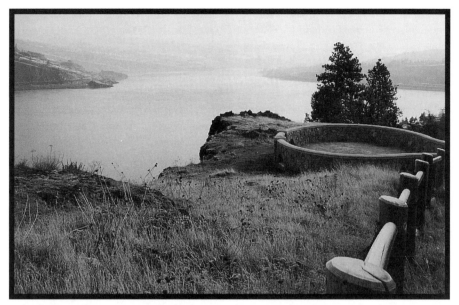

Columbia River from Historic Columbia River Highway, just east of Mosier Tunnel

lot is 0.4 mile up a gravel road to the left. To park in Cascade Locks, take Exit 44 (37 miles east of Interstate 205); the trailhead is on the left, just before the Bridge of the Gods.

DESCRIPTION

The Columbia River Gorge is one of the most distinct climate border regions in the world. The eastern end is a dry area of grasslands; the western end is a temperate rain forest. These three trails explore the gorge in a unique way, and the section from Hood River to Mosier displays the climate transition in dramatic fashion.

The most interesting section is this easternmost one. If you just want to see the Mosier Twin Tunnels, park at Mosier; from there, it's 0.7 mile to the tunnels, a viewpoint looking east on the Columbia, and a grassy picnic area beside the road. (The latter two features were added for the 2000 opening of the trail.) Here you're well into the eastern

gorge climate, where dry brush and lodgepole pine dominate rather than cedars and firs. But this scenery is even more dramatic if you start at Hood River and make the 3.9-mile trek to the tunnels.

From the Hood River trailhead, first take a quick stroll out to the lookout over the river, then duck into the new Information Center to get maps and brochures. Then start up the trail, renovated in 2000 and opened in grand style with a parade of antique cars. You'll walk through a section of firs and big leaf maples (spectacular in fall); around two miles out, a side trail on the left leads to a lookout over the river.

Just before the tunnel, you'll pass through a brand-new rock catchment structure, put in to keep rocks from the cliffs above from squashing hikers and bikers on the road below; this was also a problem when cars were on the road, especially when they got too wide and the tunnel had to be turned into a one-lane road, causing cars to have to wait their turn to enter. This fact should make you feel better: Soon after it opened, the structure stopped a 5,000-pound rock that had fallen 200 feet.

The tunnels themselves took two years to complete and had to be put in because the builders of the road got into a dispute over right-of-way with owners of the railroad below. They're a combined 493 feet in length, and they feature several adits, or windows out onto the gorge. A walkway outside the adits, part of the original road, is now off limits.

One thing to look for in the tunnel is graffiti left by a 1921 traveling party when they were trapped in the tunnel for eight days by a freak November snowstorm. It's almost at the eastern end of the tunnel, on the northern side. (They were packed for a long camping trip, by the way, and had plenty of food.)

The western section of the Highway Trail connects Moffett Creek and Cascade Locks. This is in the heart of the western gorge (rain forest) climate, with numerous creeks, countless moss-covered trees, and several fine views of the river. One of the best views is at the mouth of Eagle Creek, where road builders put in an observation area so travelers could stop and watch the construction of Bonneville Dam in the 1930s. To get there, walk north from the Eagle Creek Fish Hatchery, under the expressway for 0.2 mile. Look for great blue herons here—right under the expressway!

Just west of Eagle Creek, the Highway Trail descends a set of 62 steps and winds up on the shoulder of the exit ramp from Interstate 84—something to think about if you have a bike, stroller, or little children.

The middle section, from Starvation Creek to Viento State Park, is the least interesting, but it's also the least crowded. Starvation Creek Falls, right behind the rest rooms at Starvation Creek State Park, is worth stopping to see. The two names are somewhat interesting, too. Starvation Creek got its name when a train got stuck there by a snowstorm in 1884. Nobody starved, but after the local papers reported otherwise, the name stuck. Viento comes not from the Spanish name for wind (which would be appropriate for the area) but from a combination of the names of three men who ran a railroad there in Oregon Trail days. They were Villard, Endicott, and Tolman; hence, Viento.

NEARBY ACTIVITIES

The town of Hood River is worth a visit while you're in the area. The downtown area is compact and interesting, and in keeping with modern Oregon tradition, you should swing by the Full Sail Brewery, where they have a pub and tasting room.

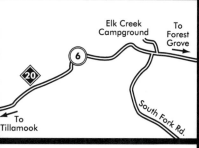

To Tillamook

Elk Creek Campground — To Forest Grove

20 — 6

South Fork Rd.

Kings Mountain

IN BRIEF

There's nothing too fancy or complicated about this hike; it's just a steep climb to a mountaintop, with beautiful flowers and a beautiful view. There's also a longer and much tougher loop available that includes Elk Mountain, but Kings Mountain is the heart of the matter in this area.

DIRECTIONS

From Portland on US 26, drive 20 miles west of Interstate 405, then bear west on OR 6, following a sign for Tillamook. Continue 26 more miles and, just before Milepost 25, park at a brown hiker sign on the right.

DESCRIPTION

This entire hike is in the Tillamook State Forest, which might not sound that impressive compared to a national park or wilderness area, but there is a fascinating story behind this forest.

On a hot August day in 1933, a fire started at a logging operation in Gales Creek Canyon. The temperatures had been in the 90s for weeks, and humidity was at an all-time low. The forest, therefore, was like a bomb waiting to go off. The Gales Creek fire started as a fairly standard fire, but then a hot, dry wind came from the east, and the 40,000-acre fire turned into a 240,000-acre fire in less than 24 hours. This "explosion" threw up a mushroom cloud 40 miles wide that rained debris two feet thick on a 30-mile

KEY AT-A-GLANCE INFORMATION

Length:
5.4 miles to Kings Mountain; 13 miles to include Elk Mountain

Configuration:
Out-and-back or loop

Difficulty:
Hard

Scenery:
Second-growth forest, wildflower meadows, a panorama on top

Exposure:
Shady on the way up, open on top

Traffic:
Moderate on summer weekends, light otherwise

Trail surface:
Packed dirt and rock; on Elk Mountain, sheer rock and scree

Hiking time:
3.5 hours to Kings Mountain, 7 hours for longer loop

Season:
Year-round, but there may be snow on top

Access:
No fees or permits needed

Maps:
USGS Jordan Creek

Facilities:
None

Very Difficult

Kings Mtn.
3,226'

Elk Mtn.

Elk Creek
Campground

Viewpoint

6

To 26

20

P

NORTH

20: Kings Mountain

1 mile scale

To
Tillamook

stretch of the Oregon coast. Three more major fires would strike, every 6 years, until 1951, by which time 355,000 acres and 13 billion board feet of timber (enough for more than one million five-room homes) had been completely destroyed. Logging came to a halt, wildlife was decimated, rivers were choked with sediment and debris, and, most important for the forest, seed cones were annihilated, meaning the forest couldn't even grow back on its own.

But starting with a bond measure in 1949, a recovery effort was launched.

Eventually, more than 72 million seedlings were planted by hand, and in 1973 what had been known as the Tillamook Burn was renamed Tillamook State Forest. Now the question facing the state is whether or not to start logging it again. Of course, you won't have to worry about that; your job is to explore one of the highest points in the forest and have a look at how the place has recovered. Keep an eye out for charred logs, for example, and remember that only 50 years ago most of this area was bare of vegetation.

This trail starts steep and gets steeper. You begin in a forest of alder and fern with Dog Creek to your right. At about 0.7 mile, stay right at a junction. At 1 mile, things get nasty steep; the next mile gains about 1,300 feet, as opposed to the mere 800 feet you gained in the first mile. When the trail makes a sharp turn to the right on a ridge top, go out to the left for your first real view to the north. Lester Creek, below you, flows into the Wilson River to your left; Kings Mountain is directly behind you. There are also some large, charred stumps on this ridge.

The last 0.6 mile of this hike gains about 900 feet, so just take your time and know that it's worth the effort. If you're here in May or June, you'll have no doubt about that when you walk past a picnic table (how did *that* get there?) and out into the meadows, which in early summer are filled with bear grass, lupine, Indian paintbrush, and seemingly a billion other tiny flowers. The summit is now just 0.3 mile straight ahead. The view stretches from the ocean to the Cascades; be sure to sign the register, one of the few in Oregon.

Now, you may have heard of this hike as part of a loop that takes in Elk Mountain as well. It is, but that hike, especially getting over to Elk Mountain, is a serious pain. But if you insist, continue off the far side of the Kings Mountain summit, and scramble along the ridge crest (where snow might linger on the north side into April, by the way) for 1.7 miles. Join a road and follow that for 1.5 miles, and then climb some of the most outrageous, crumbly, falling-apart "trail" you'll ever see, to the top of scenic Elk Mountain.

After that, all you have ahead of you is a 2-mile, 1,900-foot descent on more rocks, many of them loose. I am still the focus of resentment for sending some of my friends out on this trail without proper warning, so consider yourself warned.

If you do go to Elk Mountain, you'll reach OR 6 at a separate trailhead, but a brand-new trail connects the two, making for a 13-mile loop back to the car.

For more information, contact the Tillamook State Forest office at (503) 357-2191.

Larch Mountain

IN BRIEF

Sure, you can drive to the top of Larch Mountain, but the trail between there and Multnomah Falls is one of the classic walks in Oregon—from the shores of the Columbia River to a high lookout in the Cascades, with old-growth forest on the way up and a view from Portland to several volcanoes on top. There's even a shorter loop hike that takes in the upper parts of the mountain only.

DIRECTIONS

To start at Multnomah Falls, take Interstate 84 24 miles east of Interstate 205 to Exit 31/Multnomah Falls, which leads to a parking lot. Park and walk under the expressway to the historic lodge. For the upper trailheads, take Interstate 84 15 miles east of Interstate 205 and take Exit 22/Corbett. At the intersection with the Historic Columbia River Highway, turn left. After two miles, veer right onto Larch Mountain Road. The uppermost trailhead is in the parking lot at the end of the road, 14 miles up. The middle trailhead is 11.5 miles up on the left, where Larch Mountain Road makes a big turn to the right and a gravel road takes off to the left. If your vehicle has good clearance, you can drive 0.3 mile up this road.

Pick a clear day to take in the view; or think about timing your arrival on top just as the sun is setting—you'll get to

KEY AT-A-GLANCE INFORMATION

Length:
6.8-mile one-way with a car shuttle; otherwise, 13.6 miles out-and-back. The upper loop is 6 miles.

Configuration:
Out-and-back or one-way

Difficulty:
Hard to moderate

Scenery:
Waterfalls, creeks in wooded canyons, colossal trees

Exposure:
Mostly shady

Traffic:
Always heavy on lower stretches

Trail surface:
Pavement, packed dirt, some gravel

Hiking time:
4 hours one-way; 7 for the round-trip; 3 for the upper loop

Season:
June through October

Access:
No fees or permits needed

Maps:
Trails of the Columbia Gorge; USGS Multnomah Falls

Facilities:
Full services at Multnomah Falls trailhead; rest rooms only at top of Larch Mountain

Columbia River

84

Historic Columbia
River Hwy.

P
P
Benson
Lake

Gorge Trail

21

Lower
Trailhead
at Lodge
150'

Multnomah
Falls

Larch Mtn.
Trail

Multnomah
Creek

Rockslide

Multnomah
Cr. Spur Trail

Middle
Trailhead

21

P

P

Multnomah
Cr. Way Trail

Oneonta
Trail

Sherrard
Point
4,056'

Upper
Trailhead

P

21

NORTH

21: Larch Mountain

0.5 mile scale

see Mount Hood bathed in pink light, and the lights of Portland are spectacular from there.

DESCRIPTION

You can actually see Larch Mountain as you drive out Interstate 84: It's just to the left of Mount Hood and has a notch in the top. The top of that notch is where you're headed.

As for the hike, I confess a certain bias in favor of walking up hills as opposed to walking down them. It seems easier to recover from losing your breath while climbing than from pounding your knees and feet while descending. Still, you've got three options here, all of them quite worthwhile. You can start at the top or bottom and put in 6.8 miles (assuming you have a second car for a shuttle), or you can start in the middle and do a loop that takes in the view with less work.

For our purposes, let's assume you put a second car at the top parking lot, and we'll start at the bottom. From the Multnomah Falls Lodge, walk with the masses up the paved trail that leads over the Benson Bridge and 1 mile (climbing 600 feet) to a junction with a side trail leading to the viewing platform at the top of the falls. When you continue past this point, you'll leave 90% of the masses behind; for the next several miles you may well have the Larch Mountain Trail (#441) to yourself. You will also enter one of the few areas of old-growth forest in the Columbia River Gorge.

The trail was built in the 1910s to coincide with the opening of the Columbia River Highway—and one thing we should get straight is that there are no larch trees on Larch Mountain. The name stuck when old-time loggers confused the noble fir with the larch, which only grows east of the Cascade

Range (although they have a few in the Washington Park-Hoyt Arboretum; see page 192).

Staying on this trail, you'll cross Multnomah Creek and pass two lovely waterfalls. At 1.8 miles, ignore the Wahkeena Trail on the right. At two miles you'll cross Multnomah Creek again, then at 3.1 miles traverse the East Fork of Multnomah Creek. Just 0.6 mile later you'll cross a one-log footbridge, which, by pure coincidence, my friend Christie and I were the first people to cross. (The workers had just set the log in place and allowed the crossing before they started on the handrails.)

At 3.9 miles you'll cross a rockslide and then start climbing through an old-growth forest of western hemlock and Douglas fir trees that get as thick as five and six feet. In late summer, this area abounds with huckleberries, and in autumn the red/yellow/orange vine maple is astounding.

At 4.8 miles you'll come to a junction with the Multnomah Creek Way Trail (#444), and you'll have an option as to which way to go. Your first option is to simply stay on the Larch Mountain Trail (#441), and in two miles you'll come to the top. The second option, (#444) to the left, is a more scenic route to the top but is also 0.7 mile longer. If that sounds okay, take it for 0.2 mile until it crosses Multnomah Creek, then turn right and go 2.5 miles through a marsh and up the ridge of Larch Mountain. When you come to the Oneonta Trail (#424) at the top of the ridge, turn right and follow it 0.9 mile to the parking area atop Larch Mountain. Then follow a signed, paved trail to Sherrard Point for the big view.

Now, as for your other hiking options on Larch Mountain, you can either start at the top and go down to Multnomah

Falls (following either the Larch Mountain Trail all the way down or the loop described above via the Multnomah Creek Way Trail) or you can park at the middle trailhead described above. This accesses the upper part of Larch Mountain without 3,000 feet of climbing from the Columbia. From that trailhead, either walk up the Larch Mountain Trail 1.5 miles to the top, or go down it half a mile, take the Multnomah Creek Way Trail (#444), and take the loop described above.

Any way you go, make sure when on top that you go out the paved trail to Sherrard Point and have a look around. You'll see (if it's clear) Portland, Mount Hood, Mount Jefferson, Mount Adams, Mount St. Helens, and Mount Rainier. You'll also notice that you're at the top of a cliff on a semicircular ridge. That's because Larch Mountain is what remains of an ancient volcano, and what you're looking down into is its former crater.

Millions of years ago lava flows from volcanoes like this used to occasionally dam the Columbia River, forming lakes that stretched back into Montana and occasionally broke through in catastrophic floods. At times like this there would have been some 400 feet of water where Portland is now—just a little something to think about as you walk back to your car. For more information,

Upper Multnomah Falls

call the Columbia River Gorge National Scenic Area office at (541) 386-2333.

NEARBY ACTIVITIES

If you did the one-way car shuttle, stop on the way to or from Multnomah Falls at the Portland Women's Forum Viewpoint on the Historic Columbia River Highway. It's a little farther west than the more famous Vista House, and it is therefore a less seen view up the Columbia River Gorge.

Laurel Hill

IN BRIEF

Step back into Oregon's history on a section of the old Barlow Road, an Oregon Trail alternative to the then-dangerous Columbia River. With just a few minutes you can see a fascinating piece of history; with a few hours you can see that and more, including lovely Little Zigzag Falls.

DIRECTIONS

From Portland on US 26, drive 42 miles east of Interstate 205 and turn left on Road 2639, which is 1 mile past the town of Rhododendron and is marked by a sign: KIWANIS CAMP ROAD. The lower (unmarked) trailhead is less than 100 yards on the right; parking is across the road. For the upper trailhead (to start near the Laurel Hill Chute), stay on US 26 for 2.1 more miles and pull over at the historic marker on the right side. There's parking for just a few cars.

DESCRIPTION

It's tough to tell which is more amazing: the June rhododendron show in this area or the fact that the pioneers got through here in the 1840s and 1850s in cattle-pulled wagons. To decide, you'll want to have a look for yourself.

From the lower trailhead, you'll start up the Pioneer Bridle Trail, named because this section of the Barlow Road was so steep that travelers (going in the opposite direction) had to lower their

KEY AT-A-GLANCE INFORMATION

Length:
0.8 mile to 5.3 miles

Configuration:
Out-and-back

Difficulty:
Easy to moderate

Scenery:
Forest, two abandoned historic roadways, a nice little waterfall

Exposure:
Shady all the way

Traffic:
Light use, but beware of mountain bikers on the Pioneer Bridle Trail

Trail surface:
Packed dirt and one stretch of pavement that has cars and trucks on it

Hiking time:
30 minutes to see the chute, 4 hours to see it all

Season:
April to November

Access:
Northwest Forest Pass required only on Road 2639

Maps:
Green Trails #461 (Government Camp); USGS Government Camp

Facilities:
None at the trailhead. The water in Little Zigzag River must be treated.

22: Laurel Hill

0.5 mile scale

NORTH

Zigzag River

Little Zigzag River

To Government Camp

26

Viewpoint

22

P

P

FS 2639

Pioneer Bridle Trail

26

22

P

wagons with ropes or brake them by dragging whole trees behind—and this is what they went through by taking the Barlow Road so they didn't have to go down the Columbia River by boat.

Take a few steps into the woods and then left at a junction. Soon you'll climb the hill the pioneers came down. If you do so in June, you'll be in a world of pink rhododendrons, which the pioneers thought were laurel (they came through in the fall, when the plants weren't blooming and, judging from their journals, it rained every moment). After crossing over the top of the hill, 700 feet above where you started, you'll drop down to a point where a side trail leads to the right, out to US 26. To just head up to Little Zigzag Falls, stay on the main trail, and don't go to the highway.

If you want to see the Laurel Hill Chute, another steep (and incredibly rocky!) hill the pioneers came down, and also stay on the original route of the Barlow Road, cross US 26 and walk to the historical marker on the far side. From there, walk up a series of steps and turn right on an old road; this is the 1920s-era Mount Hood Loop Highway, which was abandoned decades ago when US 26 went in.

Just up the road, you'll see on the left the chute itself, which pioneers called "the longest and steepest hill from the States to Oregon." If you want to go to the top of it, you have two options: one is to take a steep shortcut that starts behind the sign just right of the chute; the other is to follow the more gradual trail that departs the road a little farther up. They wind up at the same four-way intersection. On the main trail, keep straight at that intersection (it would be a left if you took the shortcut) for the top of the chute and a nice view down the Camp Creek Valley. The fourth trail

at that intersection, by the way, is the original Barlow Road route, but other than that fact and a lot more rhododendrons, it's not particularly worth visiting.

Now, for Little Zigzag Falls, walk back across US 26 and down to where you came from on the Pioneer Bridle Trail, which as you'll now see is by a highway sign saying SLIDES NEXT 2 MILES. Re-enter the woods, turn right at the trail junction, and keep going straight until you get to a tunnel.

A tunnel? Yep: In the 1930s parts of the old Barlow Road were converted into a hiking trail, and this is how it went under the Mount Hood Loop Highway. To get to Little Zigzag Falls, go through the tunnel, loop back onto the old highway, and walk down the road 0.2 mile to a parking lot. From there, it's a simple walk of 0.3 mile up the Little Zigzag River, which in my mind is the perfect little mountain stream. If it's late August, you can pick some huckleberries on the way and eat them on the nice bench by the falls.

If your car is at the lower trailhead, you can save yourself some elevation by walking back down Road 2639 from the parking lot, instead of going back on the Pioneer Bridle Trail. You could also, of course, park here instead of at the lower trailhead. Or you could put a car here (or on US 26) and do a shuttle. Options abound.

For more information, contact the Mount Hood Visitor Information Center at (503) 622-7674.

NEARBY ACTIVITIES
Below Laurel Hill, Barlow Road more or less followed the present-day route of US 26. Four miles below Road 2639, and 0.2 mile east of the Tollgate Campground, there's a replica of a Barlow Road tollgate. Brush, trees, and a padlock blocked the road, and for 25 cents the gate would be opened.

Lava Canyon

Mt. St. Helens
FS 8303   FS 83   23
FS 90
To Cougar   Swift
Reservoir   FS 90

IN BRIEF

An unparalleled look at geological forces at work, Lava Canyon is also just a beautiful place to be, with several waterfalls, a dramatic bridge, some challenging hiking, and a short, barrier-free hiking loop.

DIRECTIONS

From Portland on Interstate 5, drive 21 miles north of the Columbia River, and take Exit 21/Woodland. Turn right onto WA 503 (Lewis River Road), which after 31 miles (2 miles past the town of Cougar) turns into FS 90. Follow FS 90 for 3.3 miles and turn left onto FS 83. The Lava Canyon trailhead is at the end of FS 83, 11.3 miles ahead.

DESCRIPTION

First, a little history, so you'll know what you're looking at here. In ancient times, a forest covered a deep valley here. Then, 3,500 years ago, Mount St. Helens erupted, sending a massive mudflow down through the canyon, filling it with volcanic rock. Over the years, the river cut its way through the rock, forming a canyon with waterfalls and deep cuts and towers of harder rock—Lava Canyon. Then other mudflows covered all of that, and eventually forest grew back over the whole thing.

Then on May 18, 1980, Mount St. Helens erupted again, melting 70% of its glaciers in an instant and sending millions of cubic feet of mud and rock blasting

KEY AT-A-GLANCE INFORMATION

Length:
1 to 6 miles

Configuration:
Out-and-back or loop

Difficulty:
Easy for the upper section, hard to do the whole thing

Scenery:
Waterfalls, canyon, lava, suspension bridge

Exposure:
Most of this hike is out in the open.

Traffic:
Use is very heavy on summer weekends, heavy during the week, and moderate the rest of the season.

Trail surface:
Paved, boardwalk, gravel, then packed dirt with rocks

Hiking time:
30 minutes to do the upper loop, 3 hours to do the whole thing

Season:
May through October

Access:
Northwest Forest Pass required

Maps:
USFS Mount St. Helens National Monument

Facilities:
Toilets at the trailhead, but no water

23: Lava Canyon

NORTH

0.5 mile scale

Smith Creek Trail

Smith Creek

P

Ladder

The Ship Viewpoint 2,000'

Muddy Creek

23

2,930'

P

FS 8322

FS 83

down the side of the mountain at about 45 miles an hour. That eruption scoured out the forest and rock, exposing Lava Canyon for the first time in thousands of years. As you drove in, you got a glimpse of this 1980 mudflow (also known as a lahar); now go see what it gave us.

From the trailhead, you start on a paved path that, although officially barrier-free, would require some work to push a wheelchair through. You can see here that the trees around you survived the 1980 eruption, but everything below was

wiped out. Also, look around for trees that have rocks embedded in them—that's how strong the eruption was, and this point is some five miles from the crater. The pavement will soon give way to boardwalk, and two viewing platforms give both information and dramatic views of the upper canyon.

After 0.4 mile you'll come to a junction; stay straight for now, and in 0.2 mile you'll come to the suspension bridge. It's only 3 feet wide and 100 feet long, and it was built to allow some bounce. Small kids probably shouldn't go below the suspension bridge, and everybody should be careful if it has rained recently. If you'd like to do only a 1.3-mile loop, cross the bridge and follow the trail back up; you'll wind up at the first intersection after crossing another small bridge.

For a little more adventure and scenery, follow the trail downhill (and I do mean *down*) from the suspension bridge. Just note that in the next section of trail, you'll go down steep slopes, along unguarded ledges, across a couple of bridgeless creeks, and down a 40-foot ladder. After that, you have to climb back up 900 feet in about a mile. So if it has been raining, or you're tired or nervous about heights, think twice before you go past the bridge.

After a steep half a mile down, passing several beautiful waterfalls and an area where the river flows through a chute just a few feet wide, the trail mellows somewhat. At 0.8 mile, you'll climb down a ladder (be careful if your shoes are wet!) and then cross a mossy stream. The rock formation on your right here is known as The Ship; it was one of the formations left standing thousands of years ago when the river cut a new course through the ancient canyon. The top of The Ship was the floor of the valley before 1980. There's a little perspective, eh?

You can get to the top of The Ship, and it's worth doing. A trail on the right leads 0.2 mile up it; it's pretty steep and includes rock steps and yet another (smaller) ladder, but there are late-summer huckleberries up there, and it's a heck of a place for a picnic.

At this point, you've seen the best of the hike, so it's a good spot to turn

Looking up Lava Canyon from "The Ship"

around. But if you'd like to keep going, the Lava Canyon Trail continues another 1.3 miles to the Smith Creek trailhead, losing 350 feet in elevation on the way. There's a neat bridge just before the end, another good chance to see the remains of the 1980 mudflow.

Whenever you decide to head back, cross the suspension bridge when you get to it, and take the loop hike back. You'll wind up out on a pre-1980 lava flow, with good roaming available off the trail. When you cross a small metal bridge, turn left, and you're 0.4 mile from the car.

For more information, call the Mount St. Helens National Volcanic Monument office at (360) 247-3900.

Lewis River

IN BRIEF

Here's a pleasant, mostly flat stroll along a beautiful river with three dramatic waterfalls. Chances are, they're unlike most falls you've seen, too. The long drive to the trailhead is worth it, and you can even get a remote burger on the way.

DIRECTIONS

From Portland on Interstate 5, drive 21 miles north of the Columbia River and take Exit 21/Woodland. Turn right onto WA 503 (Lewis River Road), which after 31 miles (2 miles past the town of Cougar) turns into FS 90. Follow FS 90 for 30 more miles (note that you'll have to turn right just past the Pine Creek Information Center to stay on FS 90) to the Lower Lewis River Falls Recreation Area; the trailhead is down that road and on the right. You may notice that a mile before the campground on FS 90 there's a Lewis River trailhead, just past a bridge. You can start there, if you'd like, but it adds three miles to the round-trip hike, and doesn't add any waterfalls to the view.

DESCRIPTION

From the trailhead in the picnic area, follow a trail that starts just left of the rest rooms. In 100 yards turn right to several viewpoints above Lower Falls, one of the most dramatic falls around. The water looks like it's spilling off a shelf, and in fact it is—this is the edge of an ancient lava flow. Over the next

KEY AT-A-GLANCE INFORMATION

Length:
5.6 miles

Configuration:
Out-and-back

Difficulty:
Easy

Scenery:
Several waterfalls, stream flowing through a wooded canyon, old-growth forest

Exposure:
Shady all the way

Traffic:
Use is heavy all summer long, especially on weekends.

Trail surface:
Gravel at first, then packed dirt with some roots

Hiking time:
3 hours

Season:
Year-round, although it might get snow in the winter

Access:
Northwest Forest Pass required

Maps:
Green Trails #365 (Lone Butte)

Facilities:
Toilets at the trailhead; from spring to fall there's drinking water in the campground.

24: Lewis River

0.5 mile scale

NORTH

Cooper
Creek

Upper
Falls
1,800'

Cooper
Falls

Middle
Falls

FS 90

24

P

1,520'

Lower
Falls

P

24

Alternate
Trailhead

stretch of trail, you're walking around the campground, so there are a lot of trails. Turning left will throw you off track and into the campground, but turning right will offer several opportunities to get right down to the river. Once you're above the falls there are some nice opportunities to swim.

About half a mile after you leave the campground area, look for a bridge (or, rather, half a bridge) across the river. According to the 1965 USGS map of the area, the Lewis River Campground used to be on the far side of the river, so that bridge offered access from that campground to this trail.

Around 0.8 mile from the campground, you'll pass the top of a small waterfall, and then 1.2 miles out you'll cross Copper Creek Falls, which looks like a waterslide into the Lewis River (don't try it). You may notice, on the left, two trails leading up the hill, one just before Copper Creek and one just after. This is a half-mile scenic loop you can do on the way back, if you'd like. Just

Lower Lewis River Falls

past the second of these trails, the main trail arrives at Middle Falls, another shelflike falls worth exploring for a while. Just be careful, as the rock here is almost always wet and slippery.

Back on the main trail, you'll soon pass under some enormous cliffs, then drop down into an area with some seriously large trees. There are some western red cedars here in the neighborhood of six feet thick, and one Douglas fir on the left that must be ten feet thick. Just past this area you'll come to a campsite on the right, then the amphitheater of Upper Falls, an 80-foot plunge. There are good logs and rocks in the sun here for picnicking or just general lounging. A trail to the left leads 0.2 mile up the hill to a platform at the top of Upper Falls, a very worthy side trip. Just a few moments above it, there's a view of yet another falls above Upper Falls.

On the way back, just past Middle Falls, go ahead and take the Copper Creek scenic byway. Just take the first right past Middle Falls, climb briefly to another waterfall up Copper Creek, then take a left at the fork (the road is to the right) and you'll be back on the main trail, 1.5 miles from the car.

For more information, call the Mount St. Helens National Volcanic Monument office at (360) 247-3900.

NEARBY ACTIVITIES
As you drove out FS 90, you probably noticed Kevin's Burger Buggy. It might seem out of place, especially with its drive-through option in this forest setting, but they make a pretty decent burger there, and you can't beat the setting—especially under the tent with the Christmas lights. They're open weekends only from May through mid-October.

Lookout Mountain

IN BRIEF

One of the easternmost points in this book, Lookout Mountain is also one of the widest and most wonderful viewpoints, stretching from south of the Three Sisters all the way to Mount Rainier.

DIRECTIONS

From Portland on US 26, drive 51 miles east of Interstate 205 and turn north on OR 35, following signs for Hood River. For the longer hike on the Gumjuwac Trail, go ten miles on OR 35 and turn right into a parking area across from Robinhood Campground. To drive to High Prairie for the shorter loop, go 2.5 more miles on OR 35 and turn right onto FS 44. After 3.7 miles, turn right (following a sign for High Prairie) onto gravel FS 4410. Over the next 4.6 miles, over which the road occasionally rides like a washboard, take the larger, more uphill road at all the junctions. At a sign for Badger Lake on the right, follow FS 4410 around to the left; the parking area is 100 yards ahead.

DESCRIPTION

First, the "studly" route: From the Gumjuwac Trailhead on OR 35, the first 2.4 miles will be uphill, climbing 1,600 feet to Gumjuwac Saddle and FS 3550. (In case you're thinking of driving FS 3550 to this point, you'd better have four-wheel-drive. If you insist, turn right at

KEY AT-A-GLANCE INFORMATION

Length:
2.2 or 9.2 miles
Configuration:
Out-and-back or loop
Difficulty:
Easy or hard
Scenery:
One of the great vista points in Oregon
Exposure:
Shady, exposed rock at the top
Traffic:
Heavy use on weekends, moderate otherwise
Trail surface:
Packed dirt and rock; High Prairie is wheelchair-traversible.
Hiking time:
1 hour or 5 hours
Season:
July through October
Access:
Northwest Forest Pass required at both trailheads
Maps:
Green Trails #462 (Mount Hood); USGS Badger Lake
Facilities:
Outhouse at High Prairie. There's a stream at Gumjuwac, but its water must be treated.

East
Fork
Hood
River

To Hood River

NORTH

25: Lookout Mountain

0.5 mile scale

35

FS 4410

P

25

5,860'

High Prairie

FS 3550

Viewpoint

Viewpoint
6,525'

Robinhood
Campground

Divide Trail

P

Viewpoint
4,900'

Gumjuwac Saddle
5,220'

the Badger Lake sign mentioned in the directions to High Prairie and bounce about three miles to the trail.) When you're halfway up the Gumjuwac Trail you'll reach a point on a ridge top where the trail cuts up and to the left, with a rocky outcropping down and to the right. At the top, walk across Road 3550 and start to your left on the Divide Trail (#458), following a sign for Look-

out Mountain. It will be fairly flat for a mile or so, then turn up and climb the face of Lookout Mountain. Just below the summit, stay straight when the High Prairie Loop (#493) cuts off to the left.

Now, if you're more into driving up long hills than walking up them, here's the High Prairie Loop. There are a lot of trails on Lookout Mountain, some of which are not on trail maps. So take our map with you and remember that just about all these trails go to the same two places: Lookout Mountain and the trailhead.

From the parking area, walk straight across FS 4410 and up the wide path, so well worn it's practically paved, into the meadows. The fields of daisies and lupine might make you want to stop there, but it's worth it to keep going. The trail you see immediately on your right, labeled for horses to follow, is the Loop Trail (#493) coming back to the trailhead. Ignore it for now.

Follow the wide trail ahead for 1 mile until, in an area of reddish rock, it splits into three trails. The faint one through the trees on the right is a cutoff to the return portion of the Loop Trail; ignore it. The one straight ahead (and up the hill) is the quickest route to the top of Lookout Mountain, just 200 yards up. If you stay on the wide trail, you'll loop around to the left to a point with a fine view east of the Cascades, out into the Oregon High Desert. The road then loops back around to the right and intersects the Divide Trail (#458). You can actually go left here for 1.6 miles and reach Oval Lake (turn left onto the Fret Creek Trail after 1.4 miles) and a rocky pinnacle called Palisade Point. For Lookout Mountain, turn right onto the Divide Trail and follow it 0.3 mile, past numerous cutoffs to the left for viewpoints; there's even a sort of parallel trail here that adds some confusion. Walk either one, and when you see the High Prairie Loop going to the left, stay right and you'll be on the summit.

The view from up here is one that you just can't get from the western side of the Cascades, or for that matter from most points in the Cascades. From left to right, on a clear day, you can see Diamond Peak, the Three Sisters, Jefferson, Hood (absolutely huge just seven miles

East side of Mount Hood from the top of Lookout Mountain

across the way), St. Helens, Rainier, and Adams. From Diamond Peak to Rainier, as the crow flies, is about 225 miles.

If only to see some new country, return to the trailhead by completing the High Prairie Loop. To do this, when you're on Lookout Mountain facing Mount Hood, take the trail that goes down and to your left, which is the Divide Trail coming up from Gumjuwac Saddle. A hundred feet down, take the signed Loop Trail to your right and follow it as it crosses the face of Lookout Mountain and dives into the woods. After 0.7 mile, turn right at a sign and walk back through the meadows to rejoin the wide, packed trail you started on just above FS 4410.

For more information, call the Barlow Ranger District office at (541) 467-2291.

Lost Lake

IN BRIEF

As hikes go, this is more like a resort area, with boats for rent, picnic tables with grills, a campground, and a beautiful lake stocked with trout. It's also a lovely walk around the natural, 240-acre lake, including an interpretive, barrier-free Old Growth Trail and one of the most photographed views of Mount Hood.

DIRECTIONS

From Portland on Interstate 84, drive 55 miles east of Interstate 205 and take Exit 62/W. Hood River. Turn right at the end of the off-ramp, then take an immediate right onto Country Club Road. At the end of Country Club Road, three miles later, turn left at a stop sign onto Barrett Drive. After 1.3 miles, turn right onto Indian Creek Road (the second stop sign you'll come to on Country Club Road), which turns into Dee Highway. Go 8.5 miles and turn right onto Lost Lake Road (FS 13). The resort is 14 miles ahead at the end of the road.

DESCRIPTION

Whether you just want some old-growth education or a longer walk, Lost Lake has what you need; that's why there are often so many people there. But, as is always the case, their number decreases in direct proportion to how far you walk.

For the 3.3-mile trail around the lake, start right in front of the newly renovated General Store. Walk down to the boat

KEY AT-A-GLANCE INFORMATION

Length:
3.3 miles around the lake; an additional 4 miles to Lost Lake Butte

Configuration:
Loop with an out-and-back option

Difficulty:
Easy to moderate

Scenery:
Lake beaches, a great view of Mount Hood, huge trees

Exposure:
Shady, unless you get on the lake or climb to the top of the butte

Traffic:
Heavy on summer days, very heavy on weekends

Trail surface:
Packed dirt and boardwalk; Lakeshore Trail is wheelchair-traversible.

Hiking time:
1.5 hours around the lake; another 2 hours to Lost Lake Butte

Season:
May through October

Access:
$5 day-use fee per vehicle

Maps:
USGS Bull Run Lake; free maps at Lost Lake General Store

Facilities:
Full-service camping resort

26: Lost Lake

0.5 mile scale

dock and turn right; two massive western red cedars welcome you. The first quarter mile of this trail, which parallels the road, is dotted with picnic tables tucked down by the lakeshore, each one with its own barbecue grill. After a couple of minutes you'll come to a platform with the killer view of Mount Hood. Although the mountain is about nine miles away, as the crow flies, it dominates the view from Lost Lake and somehow seems closer than it is.

Beyond the platform, the trail leaves the road, and you start to feel like you're actually out in the woods. In late August, your progress will be reduced by plump, ripe huckleberries; you can pick a handful or two to go along with your lunch, then choose a little beach off the trail to sit on a log and find some peace while you eat.

After just less than a mile, you'll come to a marshy area where the trail becomes a boardwalk for a while. After another

Western Red Cedar on the Old-Growth Trail at Lost Lake

mile, the Huckleberry Mountain Trail (#617) leads right 2.5 miles to an intersection with the Pacific Crest Trail. Just past the Huckleberry Mountain Trail, veer right from the Lakeshore Trail onto the Old Growth Trail (#657). To reach it, after you veer right the first time, stay left as you approach a group of buildings. This will put you onto a road; the Old Growth Trail begins 100 yards ahead on a boardwalk and immediately passes between two of the largest cedars you are ever likely to see. They're both in the neighborhood of 12 feet thick.

This trail is a great one for the kids because it's not too long and includes educational signs explaining the roles in a forest's life of nurse logs, the forest canopy, the weather, pileated woodpeckers, and other animals. Some of these trees are hundreds of years old and more than 200 feet tall. When the boardwalk runs out, go

another 0.3 mile, follow a trail through the campground down to the lake, and turn right to get back to your car.

To climb Lost Lake Butte for a view of, as the resort's hiking map puts it, "pretty near everything worth seeing," start in the General Store parking area. It's a steady climb of 1,300 feet in 2 miles to an old fire lookout. Mount Hood, of course, is the dominant view to the south, but you can also see as far north as Mount Rainier (but not Mt. Baker, as the resort map says). Then just come back down the way you went up and get yourself a cool drink in the store as a reward for all your effort.

For more information, call the Lost Lake Resort office at (541) 386-6366.

NEARBY ACTIVITIES
If you'd like to fish Lost Lake, a one-day license is $8.25.

Macleay Trail

IN BRIEF

If you just take the easier trip to the Audubon Society, you'll get some quiet time in the woods, including two monumental trees, and close-up views of (caged) wildlife. If you put in a little more effort, you'll get that and some history with a great view—and another monumental tree. And it's all right in the middle of town!

DIRECTIONS

From downtown Portland, drive west on Burnside Street and turn right on NW 23rd Avenue. Proceed 23 blocks and turn left on Thurman Street. Go six blocks to NW 28th Avenue and turn right. Go one block, turn left on NW Upshur, and follow it three blocks to the trailhead at the end of the road. This trailhead can also be reached via Tri-Met. From downtown, take the #15 bus (NW 23rd Avenue), but make sure it's headed for Thurman Street and not Montgomery Park. Get off at Thurman and 28th, walk one more block, and descend a flight of steps at the side of the bridge.

DESCRIPTION

When you get to this trailhead, check to see if the building there is open. If it is, take a look inside. That's the headquarters of the Forest Park Ivy Removal Project. It has cleared hundreds of acres and saved thousands of trees in Forest Park from invasive English ivy, which

KEY AT-A-GLANCE INFORMATION

Length:
2.8 miles to Macleay Park; 5.2 miles to Pittock Mansion

Configuration:
Out-and-back

Difficulty:
Easy to Macleay Park and the Audubon Society; moderate to Pittock Mansion

Scenery:
Quiet woods, predatory birds (in cages), three must-see trees

Exposure:
Shady

Traffic:
Light use on the trail but moderate on weekends; heavy at the mansion

Trail surface:
Packed dirt with some gravel

Hiking time:
1 hour to the Audubon Society; 2.5 hours for the whole thing

Season:
Year-round

Access:
No fees or permits needed

Maps:
USGS Portland

Facilities:
Water and toilets at trailhead and Audubon Society; water at mansion

27: Macleay Trail

0.25 mile scale

P

Lower Macleay Trail

Wildwood Trail

Cornell Rd.

Cumberland Rd.

Tunnel Trail

Macleay Rd.

Stone House

Wildwood Trail

Pittock Mansion

Upper Macleay Trail

Audubon Society

Pittock Dr.

Wildwood Trail

Burnside St.

Wildwood Trail

To Washington Park

creates "ivy deserts" where no native plants can survive. In this building the crews house some of their "trophies," ivy roots bigger than you can imagine such things being. Gawk, get some water, and head up the trail.

What you're walking up here is Balch Creek, named for the man who once owned this land—also the first man to be tried and hanged for murder in Portland. Small as it is, it was the original water supply for the city of Portland. As astounding as that may seem, consider that in 1987 the Oregon Department of Fish and Game discovered a native population of cutthroat trout living in it. It is one of only two year-round streams in all of Forest Park.

Keep an eye out, at 0.4 mile, for a Douglas fir on your left that is marked with a plaque as a Portland Heritage Tree, one of 235 such trees around town to be forever protected from the saw. This one happens to be the tallest tree in the city of Portland, at 241 feet, and is thought to be the tallest in any major American city. (A 255-footer in Seattle blew down in 1993.)

At 0.9 mile, you'll intersect the 30-mile Wildwood Trail at an old stone building that was a rest room until vandals destroyed it years ago. Stay straight (upstream) on the Wildwood Trail, and after a half mile you'll come to Macleay Park. Whether you're headed for Pittock Mansion or not, turn right here and walk 100 yards to the Portland Audubon Society. They rehabilitate injured owls and hawks here, birds you can view in cages for no charge; they also have an extensive collection of mounted animals and an excellent gift shop plus-bookstore. Three loop trails explore sanctuaries from here; free maps of those and all of Forest Park are available at the

gift shop. You can impress your friends by telling them that the massive sequoia beside the parking lot is actually less than 100 years old. They grow quickly at first.

To just do a 2.8-mile hike, head back to the car. To add another 2.4 miles (and just over 400 feet in elevation), stay on the Wildwood Trail by walking along the parking lot of Macleay Park, crossing sometimes-busy Cornell Road in a crosswalk, and re-entering the forest. After 100 yards, turn right on Upper Macleay Trail. This trail climbs for about 0.2 mile, then flattens out. At half a mile, check out the cool pattern on the wooden bench. Just past that, rejoin the Wildwood Trail, turning right and uphill for the final 0.6 mile to the Pittock Mansion parking lot. The home (see "Nearby Activities" below) is to your left. Wander out to the front yard, with roses and the view of city and mountains, and admire yet another spectacular tree: a European white birch that offers enough shade for a small town.

If you were on the bus, you don't have to walk back down the trail you just came up. You can, instead, walk down the road (or continue on the Wildwood Trail) from the mansion to Burnside Street, about 0.3 mile away, cross over it (quickly), and take the #20 (Burnside) bus to Downtown.

For more information, contact the Portland Parks and Recreation office at (503) 823-7529.

NEARBY ACTIVITIES
Pittock Mansion, built in 1914 by the owner/publisher of the *Oregonian* and founder of the Portland Rose Festival, is open for tours daily from noon to 4 p.m. Cost is $4.50.

Marquam Trail to Council Crest

IN BRIEF

A lesson in what makes Portland great, this pleasant trail through a wooded canyon just minutes from downtown leads to the highest point in town, where you can take in a view of four volcanoes.

DIRECTIONS

From downtown Portland, drive south on Broadway Avenue, and where it crosses Interstate 405, turn right onto SW 6th Avenue, following the blue "H" signs leading to the hospital. Stay straight through three lights in the next half mile, eventually passing two large concrete water towers on your right. Here, when the road cuts back to the left, turn right into a parking lot. You can also take Tri-Met bus #8 (Sam Jackson) to the third light, Sam Jackson and Terwilliger, and walk 200 yards to the trailhead.

DESCRIPTION

Council Crest got its name in 1898 when a group of visiting ministers met there after a two-hour wagon drive. They assumed local natives must have held many a council there. In the early and mid-twentieth century you could ride a trolley to the top and visit an amusement park. Today you can get there by car or bus, but the best way is to walk up the Marquam Trail through a wooded canyon in which it's easy to forget you're in a city of more than a million people.

KEY AT-A-GLANCE INFORMATION

Length:
3.7 miles

Configuration:
Out-and-back with a side loop

Difficulty:
Easy on the Nature Trail; moderate to Council Crest

Scenery:
Through the woods, past some impressive homes, and then a sweeping vista on top

Exposure:
Shady all the way up, open on top

Traffic:
Heavy on weekends and workday evenings but light otherwise

Trail surface:
Packed dirt and gravel

Hiking time:
2 hours

Season:
Year-round

Access:
No fees or permits needed

Maps:
USGS Portland; guides to the Nature Trail are available at the trailhead.

Facilities:
Water at the trailhead and at Council Crest

28: Marquam Trail to Council Crest

NORTH

0.25 mile scale

405

S.W. 6th Ave.

DUNIWAY PARK

S.W. Sam Jackson Blvd.

S.W. Terwilliger Blvd.

Water Towers

300'

28

P

S.W. Fairmount Blvd.

S.W. Sherwood Dr.

S.W. Greenway Dr.

S.W. Greenway Dr.

Council Crest
1,070'

At the trailhead shelter, there are two signs leading you to the Marquam Trail. If you got a brochure and feel like adding the Nature Trail, take the path on the left that says 0.7 mile, instead of the one on the right that says 0.4 mile. This leads you 0.3 mile up the creek to a junction where you turn right and enter the Nature Trail. Numbered signs along the way point out various aspects of the local flora and fauna (that's what the brochure is for) as you traverse back to the right on a flat 0.4-mile cutoff to the Marquam Trail, which leads to Council Crest.

At this junction, if you don't feel like going up the hill, stay right and you'll be back at the car in 0.4 mile (this is the right-hand trail you skipped at the trail-head). But for the best view in town, turn left and follow the trail up Marquam Gulch. You don't really need a map for this one, because you'll be following COUNCIL CREST signs at several junctions. The first is a right turn after 0.2 mile; the second is a left turn 0.6 mile later. At this point you'll start going uphill a bit. Just before you cross a road at the one-mile mark, keep your eyes peeled for an extremely cool treehouse on your left. Oh, to live in a neighborhood like this!

A couple minutes after crossing the road, and just past a left turn at a culvert, you'll see one of the classic signs of forest regeneration: a small conifer taking root on a big stump. The new tree is taking advantage of the nutrients stored in the old one. Just after your next road crossing, there's an impressive western red cedar, probably five feet thick, right where the trail re-enters the woods.

After crossing yet another road, in an area planted decades ago with May-blooming rhododendrons, you'll come into the wide, open area atop Council Crest, where couples come to snuggle and kids come to throw the Frisbee. Take a moment on the two benches in front of you to admire the view of Mount Hood and the dates of the people the benches were dedicated to: They both made it to age 98 and died within a year of each other.

Now, go up to the stone circle at the top of the park. Plaques up there point out each of the four volcanoes and give a native name for them. Also to the east you can see into the Columbia River Gorge. The view to the west goes out to Beaverton and, on a clear day, the Coast Range. But for an odd, secret treat, find the small metal disc in the middle of this stone enclosure, then stand on it and say, "Portland rocks." Almost creepy, isn't it?

Head back down the trail, following signs for Marquam Shelter, and after 1.3 miles, when you get to a junction pointing left 0.4 mile to Marquam Park, take it. That's the shorter route back to the car that you skipped earlier in favor of the Nature Trail.

For more information, contact the Portland Parks and Recreation office at (503) 823-7529.

NEARBY ACTIVITIES

While driving to the trailhead, you may have noticed a place on the right that looked like a circus tent; that's The Carnival, a longtime favorite with locals for its no-nonsense burgers, hot dogs, and ice cream. Many a milkshake has been consumed on the premises by myself and various hiking pals.

McCall Nature Preserve

To Mosier

30

29

To The Dalles

IN BRIEF

McCall Nature Preserve is in a different world from most of the hikes in this book. It's a glimpse into eastern Oregon, a land of wide-open vistas, grass blowing in the nearly constant wind, and semi-arid forests of oaks and ponderosa pine. It also has views of the Columbia from barren cliff tops, panoramic vistas of Mounts Adams and Hood, and more than 300 species of plants, some of them unique to the Columbia River Gorge.

DIRECTIONS

From Portland on Interstate 84, drive 62 miles east of Interstate 205 and take Exit 69/Mosier. Turn right and follow the Historic Columbia River Highway (US 30) through Mosier for 6.5 miles to the Rowena Crest Viewpoint. The McCall Point Trail begins at a sign at the end of the stone wall. The river-view loop begins across the highway with a set of steps leading over a fence.

DESCRIPTION

Okay, so this one is more than 60 miles from Portland, even as the crow flies. But it's truly worth the extra bit of driving, especially in the spring and early summer. At those times of the year, there is a kind of rain shroud that exists somewhere between Cascade Locks and Hood River; while it's still pouring in Portland, places like the McCall Preserve are bathed in sunlight and draped in a

KEY AT-A-GLANCE INFORMATION

Length:
McCall Point Trail is 3 miles long; Plateau Loop is 2.2 miles.

Configuration:
Out-and-back to McCall Point; balloon to plateau

Difficulty:
McCall Point is moderate due to the climb; Plateau is easy.

Scenery:
Wildflowers, the Columbia River below, oak trees

Exposure:
Wide open most of the time

Traffic:
Moderate when the flowers are out but light otherwise

Trail surface:
Packed dirt

Hiking time:
1.5 hours to McCall Point; 1 hour for Plateau Trail

Season:
McCall Point open May–November; Plateau Trail open year-round

Access:
No fees or permits needed

Maps:
USGS Lyle; map at the trailhead

Facilities:
None

Klickitat
River

Columbia River

Viewpoints

LYLE, WASHINGTON
◎

700' ◆29◆
◆29◆
P

84

**Historic Columbia
River Hwy.**

▲ McCall Point
1,722'

NORTH

29: McCall Preserve

0.5 mile scale

couple dozen different kinds of wildflowers all blooming at once.

Consider wearing long pants here;
there are ticks, poison oak, and rattle-
snakes in the area.

Start with the McCall Point Trail first
and get your exercise out of the way. The
trail, which climbs about 1,000 feet in 1.5
miles, starts out nearly flat and on an old
jeep road, winding through the kind of
open space that is so rare in western parts

of the state. The trees you eventually
encounter are oaks, most of them Oregon
white oak, and some as much as 800 years
old. The trail turns slightly uphill when it
gains the edge of the ridge, with ever
more impressive views out to the east.
Keep an eye out for Mount Adams as its
summit comes into view across the river.

The second half of the trail is just
plain steep, and after a rain it might be
slick and muddy, so add solid boots to

your clothing list. But soon enough you'll come to McCall Point, an open hilltop with a sprawling view from Mount Hood to Mount Adams; you're actually about halfway between the two peaks, each of which is roughly 35 miles away. Looking west, you can see into the gorge; just to the left of it, the high peak with the towers on top is Mount Defiance, the highest point in the gorge and a heck of a hike that's described elsewhere in this book (see page 113).

Now, you summit hounds out there might stand at McCall Point and notice there's still some more trail going south, through a notch, and then climbing again. I walked about a mile down (and then up) that trail, through some very peaceful oak stands, but technically speaking it didn't go anywhere special before it got pinched between a fence and the edge of a cliff. So my advice is to have yourself a picnic at McCall Point and don't worry about that other trail, unless you're just jonesing for more exercise.

Back at the highway, use the steps over the fence to begin the riverview loop. This wide, easy path (which actually drops 100 feet in elevation) goes out through flower and grass country to loop around a pond. Early in the year, there will be numerous other little ponds and wet areas, each supporting their own microhabitats. The small canyon below you on your left is called Rowena Dell.

When a sign reading TRAIL indicates a right turn, you'll notice another trail that keeps going straight out into the grasslands. There is another pond out there among the trees, as well as other viewpoints out over the river. But the most dramatic view is on the official trail to your right. After that trail has gone past the pond it turns right again, but a small trail to the left leads to the top of a cliff that is not for the acrophobes among us. It's a sheer drop of 500 feet from where you stand (without a railing, so keep an eye on the kids) down to the railroad tracks and the river. The town across the river is Lyle, Washington, which lies on a gravel bar left behind by catastrophic floods that ripped down the Columbia more than 10,000 years ago.

To return to the trailhead, simply follow the trail back around the pond and turn left (uphill) at the sign.

For more information, call the Columbia River Gorge National Scenic Area office at (541) 386-2333, or the Nature Conservancy at (503) 230-1221.

NEARBY ACTIVITIES

As long as you're this far east, keep going to The Dalles and visit the Columbia Gorge Discovery Center, the official interpretive center for the Columbia River Gorge National Scenic Area. Its displays range from a working model of the Columbia before and after the Dalles Dam to a Living History Center with presentations on the life of Oregon Trail pioneers.

McNeil Point

IN BRIEF

You don't have to do this whole trail to make it worthwhile; it passes through a cathedral forest to wildflower meadows and alpine ponds, then gets up close and personal with Mount Hood. But if you do go all the way up, you can see the glacial trickle that is the source of the Sandy River and hear glaciers pop and rumble.

DIRECTIONS

From Portland on US 26, drive 36 miles east of Interstate 205 to Zigzag and turn left onto Lolo Pass Road at the Zigzag Store. Go ten miles to Lolo Pass and turn right onto paved FS 1828, which is the first right at the pass. Go 3.1 miles and turn left onto gravel FS 118, following a sign for Top Spur Trail. The trailhead is 1.2 miles ahead on the right.

DESCRIPTION

This is a honey of a hike! You start out on the Top Spur Trail, which climbs gradually for half a mile to a veritable highway interchange of trails. First you'll reach the Pacific Crest Trail (PCT); turn right on it. In 100 feet you'll get to the Timberline Trail, a trail to Bald Mountain (marked with a sign reading VIEW-POINT), and another trail leading down 2.2 miles to the Ramona Falls Trail (see page 132).

To simply head for McNeil Point, follow the Timberline Trail (#600) uphill

KEY AT-A-GLANCE INFORMATION

Length:
9.2 miles

Configuration:
Out-and-back

Difficulty:
Easy to Bald Mountain viewpoint; hard to McNeil Point

Scenery:
Old-growth forest, meadows, rugged mountainside

Exposure:
Shady with a few open spots

Traffic:
Moderate use on August weekends but light otherwise

Trail surface:
Packed dirt with roots, a few small stream crossings, some rocks and snow

Hiking time:
5.5 hours

Season:
July to October

Access:
Northwest Forest Pass required

Maps:
Mount Hood Wilderness

Facilities:
None at trailhead. There's water aplenty on the trail, but it must be treated.

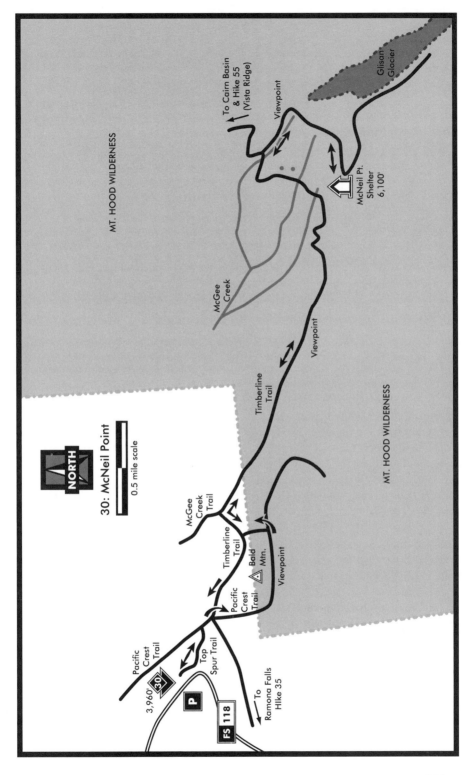

MT. HOOD WILDERNESS

To Cairn Basin
& Hike 55
(Vista Ridge)

Glisan
Glacier

Viewpoint

McNeil Pt.
Shelter
6,100'

McGee
Creek

Viewpoint

Timberline
Trail

MT. HOOD WILDERNESS

NORTH

30: McNeil Point

0.5 mile scale

McGee Creek
Trail

Timberline
Trail

Bald
Mtn.

Viewpoint

Pacific
Crest
Trail

Pacific
Crest
Trail

Top
Spur Trail

3,960'   30

P

FS 118

To
Ramona Falls
Hike 35

Strolling through the meadows on the McNeil Point Trail

and to the left. But it's well worth it to see the magnificent view from the open side (not actually the top) of Bald Mountain, a mere 0.4 mile past the Viewpoint sign, also on the PCT. Head out there to take in the sweeping view of Mount Hood and the Muddy Fork of the Sandy River. Then either come back the same way or keep going and look for a faint cutoff trail that goes over the ridge to your left, just before the PCT goes back into the woods. The cutoff goes about 100 yards over the ridge and back to the Timberline Trail; turn right for McNeil Point.

This stretch of the Timberline Trail is in a true cathedral forest—the tall, straight trees, mostly hemlocks, have no branches in their lower portions, creating a forest scene that's both open and lofty. Adding pleasure is that many of the bushes that make up the ground cover are huckleberries, whose juicy morsels are ripe in late August. You'll hardly

notice that you've started climbing in earnest.

On the Timberline Trail, at the first big view of Mount Hood you come to (you'll have gone 2.3 miles), look for the large, unnamed waterfall across the valley on Hood's flank. At 3.3 miles, you'll cross a fork of McGee Creek and, if it's August, be in the land of wildflowers. Lupines, daisies, pasque flowers, lilies, and butterflies will welcome you to the high country. Just a bit farther are a couple of ponds, which make ideal places to stop for lunch. You can skip and frolic in this area and call it a day, or keep going to the higher country.

At about 3.6 miles, just after the Mazama Trail has come in from the left, you'll reach a tiny stream flowing out of a flower-filled bowl with a snow-field at the top. If you just want more meadows without more climbing, stay on the main trail as it swings to the left, negotiate a somewhat sketchy stream

Mount Hood and the Sandy River headwaters from Bald Mountain

crossing, and connect with the outer reaches of the Vista Ridge hike for Cairn Basin and Eden Park. If you're set on McNeil Point, turn right (up the tiny creek) and follow the trail among the flowers.

About 0.3 mile up, the trail reaches the top of a windswept little ridge and then turns up it, eventually crossing a rock slide and then (in most years) a snowfield. Be careful on both these terrains; although they aren't steep, remember that even big rocks move and even packed snow is slippery. The trail keeps going up the ridge face, crossing more small patches of snow. At a junction near the top, go right for the easiest route or left to stay higher and try your skills at glissading down a small snowfield.

One mile from the turnoff at the creek, you'll reach the 1930s-era stone shelter at McNeil Point. From here the view is stupendous: Mount Hood looming above you, the valley of the Muddy

Fork of the Sandy stretching out below you, the other Cascade volcanoes beyond. As you look at Mount Hood, the sprawling glacier on your right is the Sandy Glacier and the trickle coming out the bottom of it is the beginning of the Sandy River, which flows into the Columbia all the way down at Troutdale.

Also, as you look at Mount Hood, you'll notice some more trail going up above you, into the Really High Country. It's not on any maps, but if you follow it you will (A) soon run out of breath as you approach 7,000 feet in elevation with virtually no switchbacks, and (B) find yourself on a narrow, rocky ridge between the Sandy (on your right) and Glisan (on your left) Glaciers.

I sat up there one day listening to the glaciers pop and moan as they slid slowly but relentlessly down the face of the mountain. You might even see massive boulders tumbling down the slope; you can certainly pick out their trails on the snow. At all costs, be careful up there, and most definitely resist the temptation to hop onto the snow.

You may hear or see reports of another, more direct trail between McNeil Point and the Timberline Trail, connecting with the latter at a point west of the ponds. The word from many hikers is to avoid that trail. It's steep, rocky, brutal, and unnecessary. The one described here is the only reasonable way to go.

No matter what the weather is when you start, bring warm clothing if you're going to McNeil Point. It's above the tree line, and weather changes quickly up there. For more information, contact the Mount Hood Visitor Information Center at (503) 622-7674.

NEARBY ACTIVITIES

On the way back on US 26, check out the Oregon Candy Farm. It's not, unfortunately, the mini-world of candy cane barns and sugar-water streams it sounds like, but it is a store with a heck of a selection of candies and chocolates. Go ahead: You deserve it after going to the high country.

Memaloose Lake

IN BRIEF
Not far from the city, there's a forest of cathedral-like proportions. Among those trees, there's a high mountain lake. Next to that lake, surrounded by rhododendrons, sits a picnic table. Beyond that there's a hill to be climbed, with a view of big mountains and deep river valleys where you can eat huckleberries in the sun. This is the Memaloose Lake Trail.

DIRECTIONS
From Portland on OR 224, travel 20 miles southeast of Interstate 205 to Estacada, then continue 9.3 miles farther on OR 224 and turn right onto Memaloose Road (crossing over a green bridge.) Follow this road 11.2 miles, stay right onto gravel, and go 1 more mile. The trailhead is on the left, just before a big clear-cut. If there's no parking right at the small trailhead area, there's more 100 yards up on the right.

DESCRIPTION
Take a good look at that clear-cut before you hit the trail, just for perspective. As you probably noticed on the drive, there's not a lot of the original forest left in these parts, but you're about to see some of it. Memaloose Lake is at the top of a narrow, steep valley filled with enormous trees. When you're in there, it's easy to forget that you're surrounded by logging roads, clear-cuts, and young forests.

KEY AT-A-GLANCE INFORMATION

Length:
2.6 miles round-trip to Memaloose Lake; 4.6 miles to South Fork Mountain

Configuration:
Out-and-back

Difficulty:
Easy to the lake; moderate to the mountain

Scenery:
Old-growth forest, charming lake, rhododendron blooms in June

Exposure:
Shady until the top, where it's open

Traffic:
Use is heavy on summer weekends but moderate otherwise.

Trail surface:
Packed dirt with some roots

Hiking time:
1 hour to the lake; 2.5 hours to the mountain

Season:
June through October

Access:
Northwest Forest Pass required

Maps:
USGS Wanderers Peak

Facilities:
None at trailhead, toilet at the lake; water on the trail must be treated.

NORTH

31: Memaloose Lake

0.5 mile scale

Picnic Sites

Memaloose
Lake
4,114'

Campground

South Fork Mtn.
△ 4,853'

P 31

3,460'

To 224

Memaloose Rd.

The trail to the lake is a cinch; it's neither steep nor difficult, and the scenery
is outstanding. The trees here are mostly
Douglas fir and western hemlock, two
species that grow tall and straight and
have no branches for the first 100 feet or
more. The result is an airy space with a
high ceiling—hence, cathedral forest.
The floor is carpeted with oxalis, which
looks like clover. You'll go through a
series of mellow switchbacks, then cross
Memaloose Creek; look for a little falls
back in the brush on your left. The next
switchback, to the left, is the last one.

When you get to the lake, you'll be at
the picnic table in rhododendron world.
If it's June, you might want to spend a
lot of time here among the pink blooms,
perhaps soaking your feet in the lake
occasionally. If you turn left on the trail,
you'll reach a campground on your right
(another good picnic spot); there's also a
toilet on the left. The trail to South Fork
Mountain goes this way, too.

For the one-mile climb of the mountain, just stay on the trail, which gets
brushy at times but is not tough to follow. You'll do some more switching back

before gaining the ridge at 0.7 mile; from there it's a snap to get to the top. On a clear day, the view stretches from the Three Sisters to Mount Rainier, and if it's a *really* clear day, you can make out Three-Fingered Jack and Broken Top to the left of the Sisters. Not a bad view for such an easy hike.

For more information, call the Estacada Ranger District at (503) 630-8700.

Mirror Lake

IN BRIEF

You can go a short way on this hike and join the weekend throngs at a lovely little lake that has a great view of Mount Hood. You can also put in a little more effort and leave the vast majority of the crowds behind to claim an even better view at the top of, believe it or not, Tom Dick, and Harry Mountain.

DIRECTIONS

From Portland on US 26, drive 45 miles east of Interstate 205 and park at the trailhead on the right. It's half a mile past the historic marker for the Laurel Hill Chute on the right.

DESCRIPTION

When you come around the corner on US 26 and see 75 cars parked on the side of the road, it's not a fair or something: It's the Mirror Lake trailhead. Think about starting early or going on a weekday so you'll have a decent chance for some quiet time. You'll see that the interest in this trail is well justified.

The lower portions of the trail have some rhododendrons that will bloom pink in June, and the upper portions are cool and shady, keeping you from warming up too much as you head up the hill. But it isn't even much of a hill, gaining 800 feet in 1.4 well-graded miles. Just below the lake, you'll come to the outlet creek and a trail junction. You can go either way to loop 0.4 mile

KEY AT-A-GLANCE INFORMATION

Length:
2.8 miles to the lake; 6.8 miles to the top of the ridge

Configuration:
Out-and-back

Difficulty:
Easy to the lake, then moderate

Scenery:
Rhododendrons, deep forest, a small placid lake, a big view

Exposure:
Shady on the way up, open at the lake, wide open atop the ridge

Traffic:
Heavy use on summer weekends, moderate otherwise

Trail surface:
Packed dirt, rocks

Hiking time:
2 hours to the lake; 3.5 hours to the ridge top

Season:
June through October

Access:
Northwest Forest Pass required

Maps:
Mount Hood Wilderness; Green Trails #461 (Government Camp); USGS Government Camp

Facilities:
None at the trailhead

Yocum
Falls

P

32

3,420'

To
Government Camp

Mt. Hood
Ski Bowl

Mirror
Lake
4,100'

NORTH

Viewpoint
4,960'

32: Mirror Lake

0.5 mile scale

around the lake, but if you're headed up the ridge, go right. The lake itself is a beauty. The beaches are on the right side, the campsites are on the left, and the view of Mount Hood you're looking for is at the far end, on the boardwalk in a marshy area.

To get to the top of Tom, Dick, and Harry Mountain, walk to the far right side of the lake (as you face it when you arrive) and follow a trail that goes right and slowly climbs the face of the ridge. The place you're headed for is actually right above you, but you have to walk almost two miles to get there. As for the name, it indicates the three peaks on the ridge—not, as some would suggest,

because every Tom, Dick, and Harry hikes this trail.

The trail is really just two long switchbacks, each one almost a mile long. It's time to turn left when you get to some very odd large piles of rocks, which no one has ever been able to explain. The forest opens up a little more here and, owing to the elevation, just might get you a little winded. When you get to a rocky area (neither steep nor dangerous) you're almost there.

The view from on top of this ridge is really something, considering how close you still are to the car. For starters, look how pitifully small Mirror Lake is—and how far down there. It never ceases to amaze me how quickly one gains elevation hiking. Right in front of you, looming across the highway, is Mount Hood in all its glory. Mount Adams is actually blocked by it. To the left is Mount St. Helens. What looks like a shoulder on St. Helens is in fact Mount Rainier, some 100 miles to the north.

In case you're still feeling energetic, resist the temptation to explore the other two peaks on this ridge—Tom and Dick, as it were. They're off limits because they are home to protected peregrine falcons.

Although this trail is open as early as the first of June, it will often have patches of snow on it until the end of that month, because it is shady and faces north. For more information, call the Mount Hood Visitor Information Center at (503) 622-7674.

NEARBY ACTIVITIES

The easternmost peak of Tom, Dick, and Harry Mountain is the summit of Mount Hood Ski Bowl, which in the summer is like a constant carnival. You can bungee jump, ride the Alpine Slide, play mini-golf, drive go-karts, take a trip in a helicopter, or ride the chairlift to the top of the hill and hike or mountain bike down. The entrance is one mile east on US 26.

Mount Defiance

Columbia River

To
Hood
River

84

To
Cascade Locks

Exit 55

33

IN BRIEF

Brutal—that's the best word for the
Mount Defiance Trail. But if you want to
go on a *climb,* rather than just a plain old
hike, this is your trail. Mount Defiance is
the highest point in the Columbia River
Gorge, and the elevation gain on this trail
is similar to the gain from Timberline
Lodge to the top of Mount Hood. Then
again, the view on top is nuts, so start
early, rest often, and go for it; or just take
advantage of one of the smaller loops in
this rest area along Interstate 84.

DIRECTIONS

From Portland on Interstate 84, drive 48
miles east of Interstate 205 and take Exit
55/Starvation Creek. This rest area is also
the trailhead parking lot.

DESCRIPTION

First, a little something about the name
"Starvation." In a great 1884 blizzard, a
train from Hood River to Portland was
stuck here for more than a week after
hitting a snowbank. Although nobody
actually starved, local papers reported
otherwise, and the name stuck. A sign
at Starvation Creek Falls tells the story
in detail.

From the trailhead, take a moment to
admire the lovely falls of Starvation
Creek, just behind the rest rooms. Then
walk to the west to start your hike.
Ignore the Starvation Cutoff Trail, but
look for Cabin Creek Falls at 0.3 mile.

KEY AT-A-GLANCE
INFORMATION

Length:
11.8 miles

Configuration:
Loop

Difficulty:
Hard

Scenery:
Forest, waterfalls, a high mountain
lake, panoramas of the Cascades and
the Columbia River Gorge

Exposure:
Shady most of the way up, then
wide open on top

Traffic:
Use is light at all times.

Trail surface:
Packed dirt with some roots and
rocks, some sections of just rocks

Hiking time:
8 hours

Season:
July through October

Access:
No fees or permits needed

Maps:
USGS Mount Defiance; Trails of the
Columbia Gorge

Facilities:
Rest rooms at the trailhead but no
water. The water on the trail must
be treated.

Columbia River

To
Hood
River

To Cascade Locks

84

P

33

100'

Hole-In-
the-Wall Falls

Cabin
Falls

Cabin
Creek

Warren
Creek

Starvation
Ridge Trail

Mt. Defiance
Trail

Mitchell
Point Trail

Bear
Lake

Warren
Lake

Mt. Defiance
4,959'

NORTH

33: Mount Defiance

0.5 mile scale

Just past those falls, you'll come to Hole-in-the-Wall Falls; the hole in the wall is not natural—the Oregon Highway Department did that so that the falls wouldn't run over the Columbia River Highway.

When you reach the Starvation Ridge Trail at 0.6 mile, this is one of your last chances to turn back. If you go left here, in 1 mile you'll be back at the Starvation Cutoff Trail; go down it, and you'll be back at the parking lot. But to go for the big prize, keep going on the Mount Defiance Trail. You'll pass Lancaster Falls and then have it easy for another half a mile.

Now, enough with the warm-up. When the trail turns uphill, you're beginning a stretch of 3.3 miles in which you will climb about 3,700 feet. There are a couple of viewpoints on the way, but for the most part it's just you, the trees, and the hill. When you finally reach a trail intersection, 4.8 miles from the car, you're at almost 4,300 feet—only 700 to go!

Turn right (uphill, of course), and you'll loop around the northwest side of the summit for one mile, with a view of Bear Lake below, before finally popping out at the summit. Okay, there are radio towers up there, so it's not exactly pristine—and in case you're worried, the road to them is gated, so you couldn't have driven here. The best part about the view from up here is looking south to Mount Hood or north to Dog Mountain. That hike is one of the tougher ones in the gorge, but as you now know, it's nothing compared to this one. All the folks kicking back on that summit right now are 2,000 feet below you!

To head back on the loop, go past the towers and follow the Mount Defiance

Trail. In the 0.8-mile trek, during which you'll cross a couple of roads, you'll come to the Mitchell Point Trail—the same intersection where you turned right on the way up. You can go back the way you came, a route that's shorter by 0.3 mile and not quite as steep, or you can turn right for a loop that includes a trip to a second lake. To do that, turn right and go 0.8 mile to Warren Lake, where you might want to cool your feet.

Past the lake, go a half mile, and turn left onto the unsigned Starvation Ridge Trail; if you get to a dirt road, you missed your turn. The Starvation Ridge Trail, if you don't like walking downhill, may haunt you in later years—it drops 3,800 feet in just over 3 miles, generally without bothering to switch back and forth. Turn right when you get down to the Starvation Cutoff Trail, and you're back to the car in 0.6 mile. Whew!

Call ahead for conditions—and start early. Note that there is nearly 5,000 feet in elevation gained on this hike. For more information, contact the Columbia River Gorge National Scenic Area at (541) 386-2333.

NEARBY ACTIVITIES

Now that you've conquered Defiance, treat yourself to a soak at the Carson Hot Springs. They'll even wrap you in hot towels when you get out of the tubs, and you can get a massage, too.

To get to Carson, cross the Bridge of the Gods at Cascade Locks, and then turn right onto WA 14. After six miles, turn left onto Wind River Road, following a sign for Carson. The resort is three miles ahead.

Mount Mitchell

IN BRIEF

Mount Mitchell is a moderate climb that builds suspense by keeping its amazing view out of eyeshot until the last few steps. Not that it isn't nice on the way up—especially when you get to the meadows up top—but the view of Mount St. Helens from the top is simply extraordinary.

DIRECTIONS

From Portland on Interstate 5, drive 21 miles north of the Columbia River and take Exit 21/Woodland. Turn right onto WA 503 (Lewis River Road) and travel 29 miles to Cougar. Three miles past Cougar, just before WA 503 turns into FS 90, turn right onto an unmarked road, take it 0.3 mile, and turn left onto FS 10. Take FS 10 for 4 miles (note that it turns right at 1.6 miles) and park on the shoulder where a dirt track goes into the woods on the right. If you've got clearance on your vehicle, you can drive another 0.3 mile up this road, but if you have any doubts, it isn't worth it.

DESCRIPTION

When you start this hike, you might wonder why you chose it. Take my word for it, though. The recently cut forest in the beginning will give way, and there will be views later. After the first 0.3 mile (which you may have driven), you'll climb pretty steeply, up 1,200 feet in about 0.9 mile; then you'll start to

KEY AT-A-GLANCE INFORMATION

Length:
5.4 miles

Configuration:
Out-and-back

Difficulty:
Moderate

Scenery:
Not much on the way up (it's all second-growth forest) but meadows up top and a big view of Mount St. Helens and Mount Adams

Exposure:
Shady on the way up, then open on top

Traffic:
Use is light all the time.

Trail surface:
Packed dirt on the way up, some rock at the top

Hiking time:
3 hours

Season:
June through October

Access:
No fees or permits needed

Maps:
USGS Mount Mitchell

Facilities:
None at the trailhead; no water on the trail; public rest room in Cougar

34: Mount Mitchell

0.5 mile scale

1,880'

Mt. Mitchell
4,000'

Viewpoint
3,330'

circle around to the southern side of the mountain. The next 0.7 mile only gains a little more than 300 feet, during which time things will start to open up a bit and you'll get a view off to the south, across North Siouxon Creek to an unnamed 3,300-foot peak.

Just past two miles, the trail turns right and heads uphill, out into the meadows of bear grass and wildflowers. You'll see the summit now, but what's so intriguing about this hike is that you still can't see anything of the real view you'll get from

up there. The trail eventually gets onto some rock, just below the summit, but it's no problem keeping your footing.

You might have some problems keeping your breath, however, when you get to the top and look out over the Swift Reservoir to Mount St. Helens, just 12 miles away. From here, it's easy to see the patterns of mudflows that resulted from the 1980 eruption. One of these went from the high slopes of the mountain, down Lava Canyon, and into the reservoir. Look around for more impressive

Mt. Saint Helens and Swift Reservoir from the top of Mount Mitchell

views: To your right is Mount Adams; between Mount Adams and Mount St. Helens is Mount Rainier; and behind you is Mount Hood.

Didn't see all this coming, did you? For more information, contact the Mount St. Helens National Volcanic Monument at (360) 247-3900.

Neahkahnie Mountain

IN BRIEF

One of the classic views on the Oregon coast is from the top of this 1,600-foot peak, which juts straight above the sea.

DIRECTIONS

From Portland on US 26, travel 74 miles west of Interstate 405 and turn south on US 101. The campground trailhead (where you'd park to go to the beach) is 14 miles ahead on the right. It's the third of three lots in succession on US 101. The middle trailhead for Neahkahnie Mountain is one mile farther up US 101 on the right. For the southernmost trailhead, drive 1.7 miles farther and turn left onto a gravel road by a brown hiker sign. The trailhead is 0.4 mile up on the right.

DESCRIPTION

Perhaps all these trailheads have you confused; don't be. It's really very simple: Neahkahnie Mountain has a killer view, from 1,600 feet above the ocean, and you have two options for how to get there: the express and the local. The express is a 3-mile round-trip from the southernmost trailhead; it gains 850 feet. The local is the scenic option, starting at the beach and offering more to see on the way up. It gains 1,600 feet in 3.6 miles.

First, the "express." From the trailhead, you'll switchback up through open meadows to a junction with a road that

To Cannon Beach

To Cape Falcon

Short Sand Creek

P

35 100'

P

NORTH

35: Neahkahnie Mountain

0.5 mile scale

101

Necarney Creek

Viewpoint

35

P

Neahkahnie Mtn. 1,600'

Radio Towers

P

35

To Manzanita

Pacific Ocean

leads left to some radio towers. Cross the road and follow the trail. You'll climb gradually for another 0.3 mile, pass to the north of (and below) the radio towers, and then in another 0.3 mile come to the summit. It's a little rocky scramble, but nothing intense.

For the "local," the one with the stops along the way, start at the parking lot for the Oswald West State Park campground. Walk down the trail, among some awesome sitka spruces, toward Short Sand Beach. In 0.1 mile you'll come to a junction offering a choice between beach and campground; choose beach, unless you'd like to use the rest room in the campground. In another 0.1 mile, turn left at another junction, this time crossing a wonderful, bouncy suspension bridge over Necarney Creek. Take a few minutes to explore the lovely beach, which has some pretty decent tidepools around to the left.

Now, back on the trail to Neahkahnie Mountain, you'll climb up a ridge covered with massive sitka spruces. About 0.2 mile up the trail you'll actually go *through* one of them.

When you get to the top of the ridge, you may notice there are some more western hemlocks around. These trees and Douglas firs are the only ones you'll find from sea level to higher elevations in the Cascades. When the walk-through tree is 0.3 mile behind you, look for a large western red cedar just by the trail on the left, and just beyond that two ridiculously large sitka spruces, with foot-thick branches that have turned upward and become trees in their own right. If you think they can't get any bigger, the largest spruce of the hike, with several trunks, is 0.2 mile farther along.

When you pop out into the open, in a meadow more than 200 feet above the sea, you'll have come 1.3 miles since

leaving your car. Just ahead you'll see a trail splitting off to the right; it leads to a cliff-top ocean viewpoint among the trees. Just before you reach the shoulder of US 101, you'll see another trail just like it.

When you reach US 101, cross it carefully, and start into the woods at a trail sign which, for some reason, reads NEAHKAHNIE MOUNTAIN: 1.5 MILES. Ignore that—it's two miles to the mountain. You'll climb in the open for 0.6 mile before going back into the trees. At this point, you're at about 1,000 feet above sea level. You'll keep climbing gradually after this, and then if the trail seems to be dipping downward, don't worry. You're just traversing around to the far side of the mountain, where the view is. When you come to a junction where two large trees fell, stay to the right. Eventually you'll pop back into the open and see a small trail heading up to the left; that's the summit.

From the top of Neahkahnie, you can see all the way south to Cape Meares; look for Three Arch Rocks offshore there. If it's a really clear day, you might make out Cape Lookout south of Cape Meares. The beach town seemingly at your feet is Manzanita, and the body of water beyond it is Nehalem Bay. During the invasion-scare days of World War II, the Coast Guard had a lookout up here, while soldiers patrolled the beaches on horseback and blimps from Tillamook cruised offshore.

If you chose to do a one-way hike with a car shuttle and you started at the beach, time your arrival on the summit for just before sundown. It's quite a show from up there, and even at dusk it's no problem getting to your car at the southernmost trailhead.

For more information, call the Oregon State Parks office at (800) 551-6949.

Oak Island

IN BRIEF

This nature trail—on what's actually a peninsula in a lake on an island in a river—is an introduction to the world of migratory birds that lay over at Sauvie Island every spring and fall. It also offers bountiful opportunities for picnicking and general lounging.

DIRECTIONS

From Portland on US 30, drive 10 miles west of Interstate 405 and turn right to cross the Sauvie Island Bridge. The Sauvie Island Market (where you buy your parking pass) is on your left 0.1 mile beyond the far end of the bridge. Go 2 more miles, turn right on Reeder Road, and after 1.3 miles, turn left onto Oak Island Road—although because Reeder goes to the right here, it's more like keeping straight. After 1.9 more miles you'll leave the pavement, and about 0.8 mile later you'll cross a dike. At the bottom of the dike, go straight; the trailhead is 0.4 mile ahead at the end of the road.

DESCRIPTION

Some hikes are in the wilderness, some are walks through history, some are educational, some offer a distant view. This one feels like just being out in the country. You'll even skirt a couple of crops! The whole scene might remind you of visiting your country grandparents. But even the crops are part of a plan by the

KEY AT-A-GLANCE INFORMATION

Length:
3 miles

Configuration:
Loop

Difficulty:
Easy

Scenery:
Lakeshore, woods, meadows

Exposure:
Mostly open

Traffic:
Use is moderate on summer weekends but light otherwise.

Trail surface:
Packed dirt and grass

Hiking time:
1 hour, not including lounging time

Season:
April 16 to September 30

Access:
A parking pass is required for all of Sauvie Island. A day pass is $3 (annual pass is $11) and can be bought at the Sauvie Island Market.

Maps:
USGS St. Helens; a free hiking map can also be obtained at the Sauvie Island Market.

Facilities:
Outhouse at the trailhead; the nearest water is at the Sauvie Island Market.

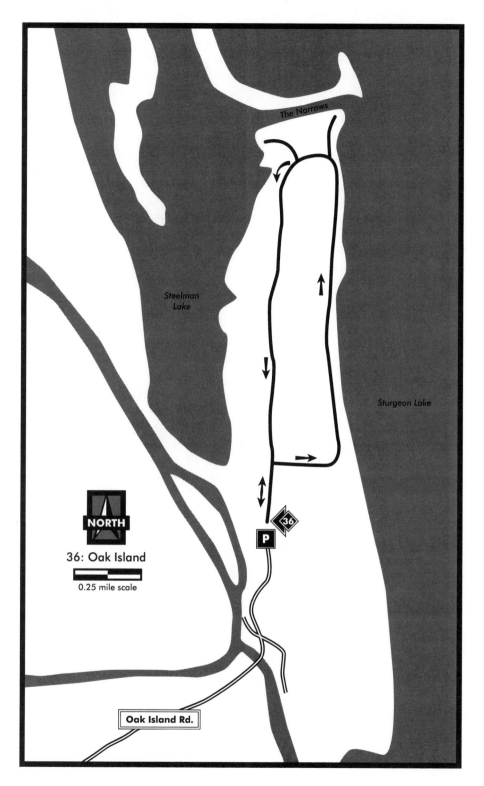

The Narrows

Steelman
Lake

Sturgeon Lake

NORTH

36: Oak Island

0.25 mile scale

P

36

Oak Island Rd.

Oregon Department of Fish and Wildlife to manage waterfowl in this area—and waterfowl is what Oak Island is all about.

For thousands of years, Sauvie Island has been a resting place for migratory birds. At the peak of the fall migration, some 150,000 ducks and geese are here. Several thousand sandhill cranes come as well. In all, some 250 species of birds spend some amount of time on the island each year, including bald eagles by the score in the winter. So if you were to go to Oak Island in the middle of a summer day, you might wonder what the big deal is. But if you come in the spring, or early on a summer day when the animals haven't hidden from the heat yet, you just might see a whole different world. In fact, even though the bulk of the migratory birds are gone when the trail is open, there are numerous songbirds here, as well as ducks, geese, and even bald eagles, who spend the whole summer.

From the trailhead, you'll walk a few minutes on the mowed roadway/trail to a junction. Along the way, be sure to grab a guide from the box; it corresponds to several signs around the trail. Go either way you want, or strike off into the grassy meadows or woods. If you stay on the trail, going right will take you to a view of Sturgeon Lake, which at some times of the year might be a long way off because it's so shallow. Turn left here, and in 0.9 mile, when the signed trail turns left, follow another trail to the right 200 yards to The Narrows, a slim body of water that connects Sturgeon Lake to the east with Steelman Lake to the west.

Continuing on the loop trail, you'll head back to the left and walk along a plowed area; the Department of Fish and Wildlife actually farms some 1,000 acres of its land on Sauvie Island as part of a cycle that brings alfalfa, corn, millet, and other foods to migratory birds in the winter and cattle in the summer.

For more information, contact the Sauvie Island Information Center at (503) 621-3488.

NEARBY ACTIVITIES

The 1856 Bybee-Howell House, the oldest home in Multnomah County, is now a museum including farm implements from the old days. It's open weekends from June 3 through September 3.

Oaks Bottom

Ross Island

← Milwaukie Ave.

Mitchell St.

Hardtack Island

37

Willamette River

Milwaukie Ave.

99E

IN BRIEF

The heart of this trail is essentially a viewing platform around the edge of a watery wildlife preserve. It's home to dozens of bird species, especially in spring and fall, and it couldn't be more conveniently located.

DIRECTIONS

From Downtown Portland, go south on Broadway Avenue and follow signs for the Ross Island Bridge (US 26 East). After crossing the bridge, turn right at the first light (Milwaukie Avenue). Go south exactly one mile on Milwaukie and park in the signed trailhead on the right, just past the light at Mitchell Street. You can also take Tri-Met's #19 Woodstock bus from downtown to the trailhead.

DESCRIPTION

It is so easy, when living in a city, to think that we are "here" and nature is out "there" somewhere, in the hills or on the coast. Occasionally you'll be walking down the street and see some Canada geese fly overhead, and you'll remember that nature is actually all around us. Whenever you need such a reminder, just go down to Oaks Bottom.

Oaks Bottom is 160 acres of wildlife habitat just a few miles from downtown. It supports some 140 species of birds at various times of the year, especially in the spring and fall migration seasons. At

KEY AT-A-GLANCE INFORMATION

Length:
3 miles

Configuration:
Loop

Difficulty:
Easy

Scenery:
Wildlife, woods, water, and even an amusement park

Exposure:
Shady for the most part, but occasionally in the open

Traffic:
Heavy use on weekends, moderate otherwise

Trail surface:
Packed dirt and gravel

Hiking time:
2 hours, but only because you'll want to birdwatch

Season:
Year-round, but it will get muddy in winter and spring.

Access:
No fees or permits needed

Maps:
USGS Lake Oswego; there's also a map on a sign at the trailhead.

Facilities:
Water at the trailhead; rest rooms and water along the way

NORTH

37: Oaks Bottom

0.5 mile scale

Ross Island

Hardtack Island

East Island

Willamette River

Mausoleum

Oaks Bottom

OAKS PARK

SELLWOOD PARK

any time of year you can expect to see herons and ducks, and if you're lucky, you might catch a glimpse of beavers, deer, cormorants, woodpeckers, ospreys, kingfishers, or bald eagles.

There are actually three trailheads for Oaks Bottom, but the one described above is the most convenient and is closest to the best parts of the park. From that trailhead, walk downhill on a moderate grade. At 0.1 mile, you'll see a wide

trail going into an open area to the right. This is a series of meadows between the main trail and the railroad tracks—actually landfill from before this was a city park. Explore them in search of birds, or spread out a blanket for a picnic. Alternatively, stay straight on the trail, cross under the power lines and over the railroad tracks, and connect with a system of small trails in the woods beyond. There are several viewpoints of an amazingly quiet stretch of the Willamette River, one of which is just above a large drainpipe with comforting warning signs of raw sewage overflow. It is highly recommended that you do not get in this stretch of the river.

Back on the main trail, you'll reach a fork at 0.3 mile. The trail to the right also leads to the railroad tracks and to the woodsy trails beyond, as well as to a collection of No Trespassing signs telling you not to venture along the tracks to the left. Staying left at the fork, you'll pass through an area that was the subject of an ivy-removal project in 2000. English ivy, not native to the Pacific Northwest, has taken over many of Portland's parks, creating "ivy deserts" where no native plants can grow. So the city went in, removed ivy from this section, and planted native conifers, especially western red cedar, in an attempt to re-establish the native plants. You can judge for yourself how it worked.

The trail crosses a bridge and begins to skirt a marsh/meadow area (depending on the time of year) of alder, blackberry, dogwoods, and reed grass—and oaks, of course. After a few minutes you'll come to Oaks Bottom proper, a large pond that was part of the Willamette River before the construction of the railroad cut it off from the main river in the late nineteenth century. What is now the park was used as a dumping ground for asphalt and other construction materials. But the area was purchased by the city in 1969 and turned into a wildlife reclamation area. The pond is best viewed in spring and late fall, when the maximum amount of water is present—both in the pond and on the trail, by the way. Bring good boots and good binoculars. At all times of the year, look for great blue herons standing still in the water, awaiting a meal, and in the summer, Canada geese swooping in for a landing on their way north or south.

When the trail reaches the end of the lake, one branch cuts off to the right and heads for Oaks Amusement Park (see "Nearby Activities" below). Another continues straight ahead to a trailhead at the southern end of the park. A third, the smallest one, climbs a small hill to the left to Sellwood Park, where there are water fountains and rest rooms. At this point, you've seen the best of the park, so you might as well head back. Consider crossing the railroad tracks and exploring those woods, or just go back on the main trail and look for more birds.

Remember to be thankful for your little reminder that Mother Nature isn't always that far away.

For more information, call the Portland Parks and Recreation office at (503) 823-2223.

NEARBY ACTIVITIES

If you hear the screams of children coming from across the pond, don't call 911 on your cell phone; it's just Oaks Amusement Park, in continuous operation since 1905. They've got all the midway thrill rides, the Northwest's oldest skating rink, and a kids' area, Acorn Acres, that opened in 1999.

IN BRIEF

Opal Creek's history can be traced from ancient times to a modern-day legislative showdown, but its value can hardly be measured. It is an almost completely preserved sample of what the Northwest used to be, a place that hasn't been logged and where the water runs clear. It's the largest such area in the state that's at a low elevation. You don't even have to work hard to appreciate it.

DIRECTIONS

From Portland on Interstate 5, drive 35 miles south of Interstate 205 and take Exit 253/Stayton/Detroit Lake. Turn left (east) onto OR 22 and follow it 22.5 miles, and then turn left onto Little North Santiam Road, following a sign for Elkhorn. In just over 15 miles, the pavement will end; beware that beyond this there are some serious potholes. Stay left at two junctions; the trailhead is at the end of the road, 5.6 miles after you leave the pavement.

DESCRIPTION

For thousands of years, the Santiam Indians had their summer camp at the confluence of what we now call Opal Creek and Battle Ax Creek. Other tribes would come here to trade such items as fish from the Pacific Ocean and obsidian from east of the Cascades. In the 1850s, colonists arrived and started mining for silver and gold. Not much of either was

KEY AT-A-GLANCE INFORMATION

Length:
7 miles round-trip to Opal Pool; 12 miles round-trip to Cedar Flats; 13 miles to see it all

Configuration:
Out-and-back

Difficulty:
Easy to moderate

Scenery:
Virgin forest and clear-water pools

Exposure:
Shady

Traffic:
Use is heavy on summer weekends but moderate otherwise.

Trail surface:
Gravel road for 3.2 miles; otherwise packed dirt, roots, rocks

Hiking time:
2.5 hours to Opal Pool; 5 hours to Cedar Flats; 6 hours to see it all

Season:
March through mid-November

Access:
Northwest Forest Pass required

Maps:
USGS Battle Ax; Green Trails #524

Facilities:
Outhouses at the trailhead in summer; outhouses along the trail and at Jawbone Flats

Whetstone Mtn.
4,969'

Battle Ax Creek

Opal Pool

Bridge

Jawbone Flats

Opal Creek

Beachie Creek

Cedar Flats

Cold Creek

Little
N. Santiam River

38

P

NORTH

38: Opal Creek

0.5 mile scale

found, but there was enough other minerals to keep mining alive here until the early 1980s. A mining town was built at the confluence in the 1920s, and it came to be known as Jawbone Flats; according to legend, while the men were out mining, the women were back there "jawboning." A sawmill was also built nearby, but it burned in the 1940s. In 1992 the mining company donated 4,000 acres of land to the nonprofit group Friends of Opal Creek, with the desire that it be preserved. Meanwhile, the Forest Service announced plans to log 15,000 acres of the Little North Santiam Valley.

This is when Opal Creek became world-famous—a massive effort was launched to save it from the saw. National TV crews visited, a book was written, and the fight went all the way to the U.S. Congress, where in 1998 the 35,000-acre Opal Creek Wilderness and Scenic Recreation Area was finally established. Today Friends of Opal Creek operates an educational camp at Jawbone Flats, and a Y-shaped system of easy trails brings visitors into the magical land of what used to be.

From the gate, you'll start by walking slightly downhill on an old road. Most of the big trees are still ahead, but there is a Douglas fir on the right (a side trail leads to it at about 0.2 mile) that is thought to be between 700 and 1,000 years old. There's a rustic outhouse at 0.3 mile, just before a crossing of Gold Creek on a high bridge; 0.1 mile past that the Whetstone Mountain Trail appears on the left. This 3.5-mile trail climbs almost 3,000 feet. If you want to see the fantastic view from up there, consider doing it on another day, starting at the other end of the Whetstone Mountain Trail (see page 195). About 0.2 mile past that trail, you'll cross over a series of half bridges; keep an eye out for an old mining shaft on the left

The road to Jawbone Flats after a snowfall

just past them. It's not recommended that you go in there.

The most impressive forest along the road occurs around the one-mile mark, where a host of Douglas firs are in the six-foot-thick range. At two miles, you'll see on the right a trail leading into an area filled with old mining equipment and the burned-out remains of the sawmill's steel and masonry boiler. Behind the one building still there is a trail leading 100 feet to a falls; it's known as either Sawmill Falls or the Waterfall of the Children, depending on whom you ask. This falls is the end of the road for a winter run of steelhead from the ocean.

Just past the sawmill site, you'll come to a fork. Straight ahead on the road there's a nice river access point on the right at 0.2 mile, then Jawbone Flats in 1.2 miles. Here, you'll find several cabins from the 1920s and 1930s, and two new ones built after a fire in 1999. (They were both built largely from wood cut and milled right on the site.) To reach local highlight Opal Pool from here, go straight through the camp on the road, following signs through a right-hand turn and past a collection of old vehicles that includes a U.S. Navy fire truck. The pool is 0.1 mile past the cars.

A long-anticipated bridge over Opal Creek is in place just above Opal Pool, enabling hikers to do a loop by crossing over to the Opal Creek Trail.

At the fork in the road, a right turn will take you across a bridge and then left onto the Opal Creek Trail proper. Several side trails will lead left to the Little North Santiam; then after one mile a sign will lead to you to Opal Pool on the left. In summer you will often see people jumping off the rocks into the amazingly clear pool. You're now looking at Opal Creek itself, probably the clearest water you could ever see and the best bet in Oregon for a stream you could drink out of. I have probably ingested two gallons of Opal Creek and never gotten sick; take that for what it's worth and make your own decisions.

Another mile up the trail, a bridge offers a glimpse down into the crystal-clear waters; there's also a great little rock pool on the far side that is a safe place for a quick dip. Another mile up,

the trail more or less ends at Cedar Flats, where Beachie Creek flows into Opal Creek and three 1,000-year-old cedars frame the trail.

I say "more or less ends" because as of 2000 the trail beyond there, to Franklin Grove, was not being maintained and was not worth the effort. The reason it wasn't being maintained is that the Forest Service has plans to relocate the trail and then build a new, four-mile section up to Opal Lake. There are also plans to connect the Opal Creek Trail with the Little North Santiam Trail, which currently ends several miles down that river. None of that work had begun when this book was written, but one day you'll be able to hike from the Elkhorn recreation area (back on Little North Santiam Road) to Opal Lake, some 17 miles one-way. Call the Ranger District office for an update.

For information, call (503) 897-2921, or go to www.opalcreek.org on the Internet. For more information, you can also call the Detroit Ranger District office at (503) 854-3366.

NEARBY ACTIVITIES

For one last look at the scenic beauty of the Little North Santiam River, stop off at the Three Pools Recreation Area on the way back to OR 22. It's 1.3 miles up from the point where the pavement ends; turn left on FS 2207, and park 0.3 mile down the road.

Ramona Falls

IN BRIEF

This trail is immensely popular, and it's no wonder. It's a fairly easy hike to a uniquely beautiful falls, with plenty of room for a picnic when you get there. There's even a side trip available for a sweeping view of Mount Hood.

DIRECTIONS

From Portland on US 26, drive 36 miles east of Interstate 205 to Zigzag. Turn left onto Lolo Pass Road at the Zigzag Store and proceed four miles before turning right onto paved FS 18, which is not marked; it's the first road after a parking area on the right. Cross the river, and after a mile on FS 18, stay right at a fork. A little more than one mile later, stay left at another fork; the trailhead is a few hundred yards ahead. Going right at the last fork would take you 0.3 mile to Lost Creek Campground, where water and toilets are available.

DESCRIPTION

From the massive trailhead parking lot, the trail is essentially flat for a little over one mile, at which point there's a junction. Either way leads to the falls; the left follows a creek, is shadier, and is probably a better way to go up. Going that way, you'll reach another junction in half a mile; stay right for the falls, or go left for a 4.4-mile round-trip diversion to Bald Mountain, with its majestic view of the northwest side of Mount Hood,

KEY AT-A-GLANCE INFORMATION

Length:
7.1 miles

Configuration:
Balloon

Difficulty:
Easy

Scenery:
A pleasant stream, soothing woods, and a one-of-a-kind waterfall

Exposure:
In the woods all the way, with occasional open spots

Traffic:
Heavy use, especially on summer weekends

Trail surface:
Packed dirt

Hiking time:
3 hours

Season:
May through October

Access:
Northwest Forest Pass required

Maps:
Mount Hood Wilderness; Green Trails #461 (Government Camp); USGS Bull Run Lake

Facilities:
None at the trailhead, but a campground with water and toilets is less than a mile away.

NORTH

39: Ramona Falls

0.5 mile scale

Bald Mtn.
Viewpoint

Muddy Fork

MT. HOOD WILDERNESS

Ramona
Falls
3,480'

Sandy
River

P

39

2,100'

Lost Creek
Campground

including the headwaters of the Sandy River. Just be warned: It's a 1,700-foot climb, and it's more easily reached as part of the McNeil Point hike (see page 102).

Heading toward Ramona Falls, you'll soon see 100-foot cliffs across the creek that have a vaguely pinkish hue. That's basalt, and the reason it's pink is that it's recently exposed due to rockfall from the face of the cliffs. As basalt weathers, it gets darker. The creek itself is a lovely little mountain stream with pools safe enough for kids to play in (so you might want to come back this way). When you catch a brief glimpse of Hood through the trees ahead—and the trail turns uphill a bit and starts to seem a wee bit tedious—you're almost there.

Ramona Falls is a perfect example of how a tiny stream can make a heck of a waterfall. The best comparison for these falls is to one of those pyramids of champagne glasses; as the water cascades over broken columns of basalt, it spreads out into a 120-foot extravaganza of water that emits a cool, misty spray into the open area in front of it. No wonder so many people come here with kids and dogs and picnic supplies! Just beware

of the gray jays that haunt the area; they'll take food right out of your hands if you're not careful.

There's a nice story, by the way, behind the naming of Ramona Falls. In 1933 a Forest Service employee came across the falls while scouting the area for a trail; at the time, he was courting a girl and named the falls in her honor. One would like to think he won fair Ramona's hand in marriage.

To complete the loop back to the parking lot, keep going past the falls and turn right down the trail. This route is a little more open, has a lot more rhododendrons, and traverses the edge of the Sandy River Gorge on its way back to the first trail junction. From there, turn left and walk just over 1 mile back to your car.

For more information, contact the Mount Hood Visitor Information Center at (503) 622-7674.

NEARBY ACTIVITIES

The Zigzag Store is still in its original 1916 building. It was originally a market and then, in 1917, the Zigzag post office. It's also conveniently located for a cool drink after the hike.

Rock Lakes

IN BRIEF

Several lakes, a flower-filled meadow, late-summer huckleberries, and a nice view of Mount Hood await on this popular loop hike, which is just one of several options in the area. You can visit mountain lakes here with just over one mile of walking.

DIRECTIONS

From Portland on OR 224, travel 44 miles southeast of Interstate 205, through the town of Estacada, to the ranger station at Ripplebrook. Half a mile past the ranger station, turn left onto FS 57. Follow FS 57 for 7.6 miles, and turn left onto FS 58. After 7.1 miles, turn left onto FS 4610, and 1.3 miles later go left onto FS 4610-240, which is marked simply "240." This is where the road gets rough and narrow; the trailhead is 4.4 miles ahead, at the end of the road, just past the campground. If your car is low to the ground, think about going someplace else.

DESCRIPTION

The recommended loop here is just one of several options from the trailhead. You could, for example, take trail #700 down 1.3 miles to Shellrock Lake, and then another 1 mile to Hideaway Lake. But this loop is the most popular one in the area, because it takes in several lakes and a variety of scenery.

KEY AT-A-GLANCE INFORMATION

Length:
7.7 miles

Configuration:
Loop

Difficulty:
Moderate

Scenery:
Lakes, a meadow, a historic cabin, and a view of Mount Hood

Exposure:
Shady most of the way, with occasional open spots

Traffic:
Use is moderate on summer weekends but light otherwise.

Trail surface:
Packed dirt with roots and rocks

Hiking time:
5 hours

Season:
July through October

Access:
Northwest Forest Pass required

Maps:
Green Trails #492 (Fish Creek Mt.) and #493 (High Rock)

Facilities:
None at the trailhead. The water on the trail must be treated.

FS 4610-240

40

NORTH

40: Rock Lakes

0.5 mile scale

Shellrock Lake

Lower Rock Lake

Middle Rock Lake

Upper Rock Lake

Cache Lake

Cripple Creek

Serene Lake

From the trailhead, take the Serene Lake Trail (#512)—and ignore the mileage listed on the signs. As of 2000, it had been wrong for several years. In 0.8 mile, you'll come to a trail junction; go left a couple hundred yards to Middle Rock Lake. From the campsite there, turn right, cross the creek, walk to the far end of the lake, and then go up the hill a short ways to Upper Rock Lake, the smallest of the three.

Back at the main trail (in other words, had you not turned left for Middle Rock Lake), go another 0.1 mile and you'll come to a trail leading right to Lower Rock Lake. All these lakes are stocked with trout, by the way, so if you're into fishing, get a license and bring your rod. If you've got small kids, or you feel done for the day, you can go back to the car now, and you will have done less than two miles. For an even nicer lake, and then some, keep going.

It's 2.1 up-and-down miles to Serene Lake, which is nothing short of lovely. Fishermen pull 15-inch trout from its deep, cold, green water. The same boulders, grassy shallows, downed trees, and thickly vegetated shoreline that hide the fish also make for outstanding scenery for humans. Turn left at a junction for campsites that also serve as perfect spots for a picnic. That trail also leads onward on the loop.

Beyond Serene Lake, the trail climbs about 500 feet in 0.8 mile to the top of a ridge and a junction with the Grouse Point Trail (#517). Turn left; in 1.8 miles you'll reach Cache Meadow, but not before seeing some fantastic views back down to Serene Lake with Mounts Hood, Adams, Rainier, and St. Helens beyond. Some of the best views are from a one-acre clear-cut, which was put in for helicopters to land in and drop off firefighters.

When you get to flower-filled Cache Meadows, you'll find an intersection. You can go right to explore Cripple Creek and the tiny lake in the meadow, or turn left and go 200 yards to the old shelter. But don't go stomping around in the meadow, as the flowers are very fragile. To complete the loop, keep going past the shelter for 300 yards, turn left onto trail #517, and take it 1 mile until you come to an abandoned fire road. Turn right again, and in one mile you'll be back at the car.

For more information, call the Clackamas Ranger District office at (503) 630-4256.

Saddle Mountain

IN BRIEF

The highest point in northwest Oregon, Saddle Mountain is also one of the most popular hiking trails in the state. That's because it's easy to get to, goes through flower-filled meadows unparalleled in this part of the state, and has a view on top that stretches from the ocean, to the mouth of the Columbia River, to the Cascades.

DIRECTIONS

From Portland on US 26, travel 66 miles west of Interstate 405 and turn right at a sign for Saddle Mountain State Park. The trailhead is seven miles ahead, at the end of the road.

DESCRIPTION

Saddle Mountain just doesn't seem to belong in its surroundings. It's the highest point in this part of the state, but the other hills around it aren't even close. It doesn't even look like them, with its two-headed, rocky summit of "pillow lava," which looks like that because it erupted underwater, millions of years ago when this area was the sea floor. Then, when you get on top of it, you might think you're on Mount Hood, with the far-away views and the wildflowers all over. Of course, with the crowds on summer weekends, you might think you're in Forest Park right after 5 p.m. on a weekday. Whatever—it's a

KEY AT-A-GLANCE INFORMATION

Length:
5.2 miles

Configuration:
Out-and-back

Difficulty:
Hard

Scenery:
Deep forest, wildflowers, panoramic view

Exposure:
In the forest, then out in the open on top

Traffic:
Use is very heavy on summer weekends, heavy on other summer days, and moderate otherwise.

Trail surface:
Packed dirt with rocks, then just rock

Hiking time:
3.5 hours

Season:
Year-round, but it does get snow in the winter

Access:
No fees or permits needed

Maps:
USGS Saddle Mountain

Facilities:
Toilets at the trailhead but no water there or anywhere on the trail

Saddle
Mtn.
3,283'

NORTH

41: Saddle Mountain

0.125 mile scale

P

41
1,660'

To
26

Viewpoint

Viewpoint

great hike, so start early in the morning and get there ahead of everybody else.

When you get out of your car, you might find yourself feeling a little intimidated as you look up at the mountain. You might even see some speck-sized people up there. The good news is, you'll be up there soon enough; the bad news is, that's not the summit.

Things start out mellow, in a young forest filled with big, old stumps—relics of logging in the 1920s and fires in the

1930s. After 0.2 mile, you'll see a side trail to the right, which leads 0.1 mile to a great view. Then you'll start climbing, gaining about 1,600 feet in the next 1.4 miles. Then you'll contour briefly to the right—catch your breath—before climbing another 400 feet in about 0.3 mile. When the trail turns back to the left and stays flat, you'll be at 2,900 feet, just 300 feet below the summit.

Now you're out in the flower meadows. There are several rare species here, like the Saddle Mountain saxifrage and Saddle Mountain bittercress—species that survived here during the last Ice Age. Stay on the trail and on the footbridges, and remember it's against the rules to pick flowers. You'll drop down briefly and cross the saddle—this is the point you could see from the car, which is now very small on your left—and then climb the last, steep scramble to the summit.

On a clear day, you can see from the volcanoes of the Cascades to the Pacific, and the mouth of the Columbia just beyond Astoria to the north. On a *really* clear day, you can make out the mountains of the Olympic Peninsula beyond that.

For more information, contact the Oregon State Parks office at (800) 551-6949.

NEARBY ACTIVITIES

A few miles before the turnoff from US 26, no doubt you noticed Camp 18. How could you not? It might look like a logging museum, and it is, but it's also a restaurant with a famously filling Sunday buffet. It's served from 10 a.m. to 2 p.m.,

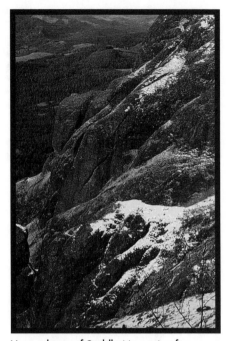

Upper slopes of Saddle Mountain after a spring snow shower

and it includes prime rib! As one newspaper story put it, at Camp 18 "you can throw on one serious feedbag." It's not a bad way to prepare for an assault on Saddle Mountain.

Salmon Butte

IN BRIEF
This easy-to-get-to trail is a mellow climb through old-growth forest and giant rhododendrons to a viewpoint that takes in Mount Hood, Mount Jefferson, and the heart of the Salmon-Huckleberry Wilderness.

DIRECTIONS
From Portland on US 26, drive 36 miles east of Interstate 205 and turn right onto Salmon River Road, which is 0.1 mile before the Zigzag Store on the left. Stay straight on this road for 6.5 miles; you'll come to a small parking area on the left and a very small road entering the trees on the right. If you have any concerns about the clearance on your car, park on the left and walk up the last 100 yards of the rough road to the trailhead.

DESCRIPTION
This trail is so well graded, you'll hardly notice you're going uphill, except for occasional views down the valley or up toward the peak. Other trails might climb similar elevation in half the distance, but they'll leave you more tired. So this is a perfect way to get on top of something without spending the whole day or wearing yourself out.

The trail starts out through an area that was clear-cut 30 years ago, so there's not much in the way of old trees, but soon enough you get into the hemlocks and moss-draped Douglas firs—and some

KEY AT-A-GLANCE INFORMATION
Length:
8.6 miles

Configuration:
Out-and-back

Difficulty:
Moderate

Scenery:
Pleasant forest on the way up, panoramic view on top

Exposure:
Shady with occasional open spots, then wide open on top

Traffic:
Moderate on weekends, light otherwise

Trail surface:
Packed dirt, some rocks at the top

Hiking time:
4 hours

Season:
June through October

Access:
Northwest Forest Pass required

Maps:
Salmon-Huckleberry Wilderness

Facilities:
None at the trailhead

Special comments:
June is the best time for this hike; that's when the rhododendrons are in bloom.

42: Salmon Butte

0.5 mile scale

2,040'

Viewpoint

Viewpoint
4,150'

Salmon Butte
4,877'

seriously large rhododendrons. At 1.3 miles, you'll come to an area at the end of a ridge with a view to the top of the butte. Just under two miles up, a trail to the right at a switchback leads to a steep, wildflower-filled meadow with a perfect rock for a photo opportunity. Around three miles up, you'll come to another open area loaded with rhodies and a view to the left of the sweeping Salmon River Valley. You'll now have climbed 2,100 of the 2,800 feet in your hike.

Near the top, the trail dead ends into an old road that once served a lookout tower; turn right and follow the road to the top, which is reached by a rocky scramble of about 100 feet. From here you're looking south and east, with Mount Hood 15 miles to your left, Mount Jefferson 35 miles to your right, and Mounts Adams and Rainier off on the horizon. In front of you is the Salmon-Huckleberry Wilderness; what a difference a lack of clear-cuts makes, eh?

While you're on top, look around for old pieces of glass and metal that were part of the burned-down lookout tower. Then cruise back down the same gentle grade you came up. For more information, call the Mount Hood Visitor Information Center at (503) 622-7674.

NEARBY ACTIVITIES

The Mount Hood Brewing Company in Government Camp (ten miles east on US 26) serves good pizza and generally has about six of their own beers on tap, with cool names like Cloud Cap Amber and Ice Axe IPA.

Salmon River

IN BRIEF

The Salmon River, which starts on the slopes of Timberline Ski Area, is the only river in the lower 48 states to be classi-fied as a Wild and Scenic River from its headwaters to its mouth. There are three sections of trail along it, two of which are described here. They are extremely easy to get to, and in the fall they host spawn-ing salmon. The uppermost section, accessed by a different road, is less inter-esting than these, tougher to find, and not worth the effort.

DIRECTIONS

From Portland on US 26, drive 36 miles east of Interstate 205 and turn right onto Salmon River Road, which is 0.1 mile before the Zigzag Store on the left. Stay straight on this road for 2.7 miles to the lower trailhead (just beyond the Mount Hood National Forest sign), or for 4.9 miles to the upper trailhead, at a bridge over the river.

DESCRIPTION

Start with the lower, easier section. From the roadside parking area (the first one you came to while driving in), you'll start out downhill through a beautiful forest of Douglas firs and western red cedars. You'll be close to the river after 0.1 mile and stay there most of the rest of the way. After two little footbridges over side creeks, you'll come to the first of several trails leading down to the

KEY AT-A-GLANCE INFORMATION

Length:
The lower section is 5.2 miles round-trip; the middle section is 7.2 miles round-trip.

Configuration:
Out-and-back

Difficulty:
Easy to moderate

Scenery:
Old-growth forest; spawning salmon in the spring and fall

Exposure:
Shady

Traffic:
Use is heavy all summer long and extremely heavy on weekends.

Trail surface:
Packed dirt with rocks and roots

Hiking time:
2 hours for the lower loop; 3.5 hours for the upper

Season:
Year–round

Access:
Northwest Forest Pass required

Maps:
USFS Salmon-Huckleberry Wilderness

Facilities:
None at trailheads; water and toilets at Green Canyon campground

To 26

43

P

Salmon
River

Salmon River Rd.

P

43

NORTH

43: Salmon River

0.5 mile scale

Salmon
River

Campsites

Bighorn
Creek

Viewpoint

river. You will pass two more small bridges, and in 0.3 mile you'll come to a campsite with a log that sticks out over the river. It's perfectly sturdy, but be sure of your balance before you go out on it.

The best thing about this trail, other than its convenience and the river itself, is the nature of the old-growth forest. Look for "nurse" logs, which have fallen and are now the home of new trees. Just past the campsite with the suspended log, you'll go up a set of steps, at the top of which there's an absolutely massive western red cedar; you can't miss it, as it's right next to the trail and about ten feet thick. At about the one-mile mark, look for a hollowed-out cedar stump with a new tree growing from it; just past it is the biggest Douglas fir (about eight feet thick) on this stretch of the river.

At about the 1.5-mile mark, you'll come to the first of two sections where the trail joins the road for a brief time. On this first one, you want to take the second trail back into the woods; the first trail is used by anglers and only leads to the river. About 50 yards off the road, look for three large trees—two firs and a cedar—almost bonded together. Just past here, where a downed tree lies along the bank, I came across several spawning salmon on a late September hike. They were in the shallows just a few feet from shore. The fish will actually go several miles farther upstream; if you hike the upper section of this trail in the fall, you'll get more chances to see them.

The last highlights of this trail are of the forest and river. One is a cedar tree so large that a hollowed-out area in its base is big enough to be called a cave. The other is a "nurse" log, cut into three pieces for trail-construction purposes, which is now host to no fewer than eight cedar saplings.

Just after a second section on the roadside, you'll drop back into the woods for another brief spell before emerging at the upper trailhead, where the road crosses the river.

Now, for the upper section. From the trailhead, walk upstream through a forest of Douglas fir. Just less than a half mile up, you'll pass a deep pool where fishermen often gather. A little while past this, when you get another view of the river from about 40 feet above it, look (in September and October) for dark shapes swirling about in the pools. Those are salmon; the black-gray ones are Chinook, and the less often seen gold ones are Cohos. Consider that they have spent their lives in the ocean and have swum all the way up the Columbia River some 75 miles, about 41 miles up the Sandy, then about 20 miles up the Salmon.

At the two-mile mark, a series of campsites on the right offer yet more chances to get close to the river and look for fish. After this, you'll embark on just about your only climb of the day, picking up about 600 feet in 1.6 miles to an overlook of the Salmon River Canyon. Just be very careful around here, and don't try any of the trails going down toward the river. You might go down farther and faster than you ever intended.

That scenic view is your recommended turnaround, as you're now 3.6 miles from the upper trailhead, but the trail actually goes another 10.8 miles upstream to a road near Trillium Lake. But at this point you've seen the best of it, so head back.

For more information, you can contact the Mount Hood Visitor Information Center at (503) 622-7674.

Silver Falls State Park

IN BRIEF

If it's waterfalls you're after—especially the chance to get behind them—this is the hike of your dreams. It's an easy loop that's commonly known as the Trail of Ten Falls. There are also shorter loops available, all of which take in views of one or more waterfalls.

DIRECTIONS

From Portland on Interstate 5, drive 17 miles south of Interstate 205 and take Exit 271/Woodburn. Turn left and follow OR 214 for 14 miles to Silverton. Note that you'll be turning right at 2.7 miles, then left at 3.9 miles. Both intersections have signs, but they could still be missed. In Silverton, follow signs for Silver Falls State Park, staying on OR 214 for 15 more miles. After entering the park, continue on OR 214 for 2.3 miles and park on the right at the South Falls parking area.

DESCRIPTION

This is the crown jewel of the Oregon State Parks system; it's also the most visited park in the state. Unless it's a rainy weekday in the winter, you probably won't be close to alone here, but it hardly matters. It's one of the finest walks around, especially if you're into waterfalls. By the way, Silver Creek was named not for its color but for a pioneer who settled here in the 1840s. He was known as "Sil-

KEY AT-A-GLANCE INFORMATION

Length:
Up to 7.5 miles

Configuration:
Loop

Difficulty:
Easy

Scenery:
Every type of waterfall in a forested canyon

Exposure:
Shady all the way

Traffic:
Use is heavy all spring and summer; otherwise, it's moderate or light.

Trail surface:
Pavement, gravel, and packed dirt; some falls are wheelchair-accessible.

Hiking time:
3 hours to hike the whole thing

Season:
Year-round, but wet in winter and spring with occasional snow

Access:
$3 day-use fee per vehicle

Maps:
USGS Drake Crossing; free maps are available in the South Falls Lodge at the trailhead.

Facilities:
Water, rest rooms, snack bar, and gift shop at the trailhead

Upper North Falls

North Falls

Rim Trail

Twin Falls

Winter Falls

Double Falls

Middle North Falls

Drake Falls

Lower North Falls

North Fork Silver Creek

Silver Creek

Canyon Trail

Ridge Trail

Lower South Falls

South Fork Silver Creek

South Falls

Rim Trail

SR 214

44

NORTH

0.5 mile scale

44: Silver Falls State Park

ver" Smith because it was said he brought a bushel of silver dollars with him from back east.

At the trailhead, be sure to visit the South Falls Lodge, built of native stone and wood by the Civilian Conservation Corps (CCC) in 1941. You can warm yourself by two massive fireplaces, enjoy photos of the park and some of the tools used by the CCC, and take advantage of that most modern of conveniences, a snack bar with an espresso stand.

With your hot drink in hand, walk toward 177-foot South Falls, take in the view from the top, and contemplate the fact that in the 1920s a man used to send old automobiles over the falls as a Fourth of July stunt. It's said that fishermen pulled car parts out of the pool for decades. Now, take the trail behind the sign. (*Note:* This is as far as your dogs can go, even if they're on a leash.) The trail will switchback down for 0.2 mile, then go behind South Falls. The cavelike setting was created over the millennia, when water seeped through the rocks above, froze and expanded, and then cracked away the rocks which now lie at your feet.

When the trail comes to a bridge 100 yards later, you can cross it and make it a day with a 0.4-mile loop. It's the first of several opportunities to cut the loop short. But keep going for 0.8 mile to see 93-foot Lower South Falls. Just before you get there, you'll see a trail plunging down to the right; that one goes to the top of the falls, but beware that there's no rail to keep you from a fearsome fall. The main trail descends a number of steps, often wet even in summer, and passes behind Lower South Falls, a combination of curtain and cascade falls.

In 0.3 mile you'll come to your second chance to cut the loop short. Turn right, and it's 1 mile along the Ridge Trail back to the lodge; stay straight, and

Lower South Falls in Silver Falls State Park

it's 1 mile to Lower North Falls, a 30-foot slide. At this point you've left the South Fork of Silver Creek for the North Fork; the two combine downstream of you to form Silver Creek—this is why you're suddenly walking upstream, rather than down. Keep an eye out for deer and beaver, both of which live in the park. Human tree-cutters left their mark, too; on some of the big cedar stumps you can still make out springboard slots, where loggers stood to cut the trees by hand.

Just past Lower North Falls, make sure to go left for a 0.1-mile side trip to see Double Falls, at 178 feet. Its shallow splash pool, which you can get in if you'd like, almost always hosts a rainbow when the sun is out. Back on the main trail, in the next 0.6 mile you'll pass 27-foot Drake Falls (named for a photographer whose images were instrumental in the creation of the park), and 103-foot Middle North Falls, which you can also go behind. When you get to the bridge (the halfway point for the full loop), you can turn right for one last chance to cut the loop short. Take this trail for half a mile to Winter Falls, and then continue past it, turn right onto the Rim Trail for 1.6 miles back to the lodge, and your day is done at 5.1 miles.

If you ignore the bridge and stay straight, in 0.3 mile you'll come to 31-foot Twin Falls, which at low water times of the year is just one falls, but which does have the hike's best picnic spot, right at the creek's edge. After another 0.9 mile (look for the rocks in the creek with ferns growing on top!), you come to North Falls, which you'll see coming for a while before you get there and which is probably the most spectacular falls in the park. Once again, the trail takes you behind the falls. Back there, look for the columns in the rock overhead, left when lava cooled around trees and then the trees rotted—15 million years ago!

After that, you have the only climb of any significance, up some steps to gain a couple hundred feet or so, then along a railing with another view back down to North Falls. When you get to the Rim Trail on the right, go ahead and put in the 0.4-mile loop to Upper North Falls, a seldom-visited 65-foot drop in an area with ample opportunity to wander around on the rocks.

On the Rim Trail's 2.5-mile trip back to the lodge, you'll pass by the top of Winter Falls, more of a damp spot in the late summer and fall, and through some pleasant forest where I have encountered deer on three occasions. When you get to the picnic area and road, stay right and you'll be back at the lodge. We recommend another coffee drink.

Dogs, even on a leash, are not allowed on the Canyon Trail. For more information, contact the Silver Falls State Park office at (503) 873-8681.

NEARBY ACTIVITIES

Just upstream from the parking area, there's an official swimming area in Silver Creek. The kids should love it, and if it's a hot day, grown-ups could probably use a dip in the creek as well.

Mt. St. Helens
National Volcanic
Monument
Headquarters

FS 5701

503

45

N.E. Healy Rd.

To
Amboy

FS 57

Siouxon Creek

IN BRIEF

An easy, pleasant stroll along a mountain stream, with old-growth forest all around and waterfalls up above. What more could you want? Even the kids will like it; with supervision, they could go for a swim.

DIRECTIONS

From Portland on Interstate 205, drive three miles north of the Columbia River and take Exit 30/Orchards. Turn right onto WA 500, which turns into WA 503 in 0.9 mile (follow signs for Battle Ground). Stay on WA 503 for 25 miles, passing through the town of Amboy. Just past the Mount St. Helens National Volcanic Monument headquarters, turn right onto NE Healy Road. Go 9.3 miles on NE Healy and turn left (uphill) on FS 57. After 1.2 miles on FS 57, turn left onto FS 5701. The trailhead is 3.8 miles ahead, at the end of the road.

DESCRIPTION

The only thing spectacular about this hike is how easy and scenic it is. There are no panoramic viewpoints, no exotic geological features, and no serious hiking challenges. It's just a beautiful river in a peaceful, lush, tree-filled canyon, with waterfalls all over the place and not too many hikers.

From the trailhead, you'll walk downhill briefly and cross West Creek on a log bridge. At this point, Siouxon Creek will

KEY AT-A-GLANCE INFORMATION

Length:
7.8 miles

Configuration:
Out-and-back

Difficulty:
Moderate, but only because of the distance

Scenery:
Old-growth forest, waterfalls, pools in the river

Exposure:
Shady all the way

Traffic:
Use is moderate on summer weekends but light otherwise.

Trail surface:
Packed dirt with some rocks and roots

Hiking time:
3 hours

Season:
Year-round, but muddy in winter and spring with occasional snow

Access:
Northwest Forest Pass required

Maps:
Green Trails #396 (Lookout Mountain)

Facilities:
None at the trailhead. The water on the trail must be treated

45: Siouxon Creek

0.5 mile scale

Chinook Creek

Chinook Falls

Siouxon Creek

Wildcat Creek

Horseshoe Ridge Trail

Horseshoe Creek

Horseshoe Falls

Horseshoe Ridge Trail

West Creek

P

45

FS 5701

be far enough below you that getting to it isn't worth the effort; that chance will come later. At 0.9 mile you'll see, on the right, the Horseshoe Ridge Trail. Ignore it. After 1.4 miles the trail crosses Horseshoe Creek (so named because it drains a horseshoe-shaped ridge, of which you're crossing the open mouth). There will be a waterfall above and below you here; to get a view of the lower one, take a side trail to the left just after the bridge.

Over the next 0.3 mile you'll climb slightly to a viewpoint of Siouxon Falls, which could almost be called a really big rapid as opposed to a classic falls. Then the trail traverses along flat for half a mile, some 200 feet above the creek, before dropping to its side for half a mile. This is where some swimming might happen—just know that it would be brief, unless you're part polar bear.

When a trail comes in from the right (the second appearance of the Horseshoe Ridge Trail), you've gone three miles. Go another 0.7 mile and you'll come to an unnamed creek on the right and a nice new bridge over Siouxon Creek, which at this point flows through a narrow gorge. Cross the bridge and go 0.3 mile to beautiful, 50-foot Chinook Creek

Chinook Falls at the upper end of the Siouxon Creek hike

Falls. Sit down here or back at the bridge for a snack, and then head back to the car. Simple but beautiful, wasn't it?

For more information, contact the Mount St. Helens National Volcanic Monument office at (360) 247-3900.

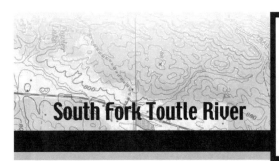

South Fork Toutle River

IN BRIEF

Without driving all the way around to the other side of Mount St. Helens, this is the most dramatic view you can get of the results of that mountain's 1980 eruption. A major mudflow went all the way down the Toutle River to the Columbia, where shipping was stopped for days while the debris was dredged out. This hike will show you the South Fork of that river, where the mudflow was half a mile wide, as well as a glimpse of the majesty which the eruption destroyed.

DIRECTIONS

From Portland on Interstate 5, drive 21 miles north of the Columbia River and take Exit 21/Woodland. Turn right onto WA 503 (Lewis River Road) and travel 28 miles; then turn left onto FS 8100, following a sign for Merrill Lake. Travel 11.5 miles on FS 8100, and then stay straight at a junction, which puts you on FS 8123. The trailhead is at the end of FS 8123, 6.4 miles ahead.

DESCRIPTION

From the trailhead, things will be easy for the first 0.6 mile, giving you a chance to get warmed up. After that, you get to a rock cairn, marking a trail junction. To the left the trail leads across a bridge that spans Sheep Canyon; that's the way you'll be coming back. For the loop, keep going straight and start climbing gradually through a lovely

KEY AT-A-GLANCE
INFORMATION

Length:
7 miles

Configuration:
Loop

Difficulty:
Hard

Scenery:
Old-growth forest, waterfalls in canyons, flower-filled meadows

Exposure:
Most of the hike is shady until the end when you'll be out in the open.

Traffic:
Use is moderate on summer weekends but light otherwise.

Trail surface:
Packed dirt with rocks and roots in most places; some areas are just rock.

Hiking time:
4 hours

Season:
June through October

Access:
Northwest Forest Pass required

Maps:
USFS Mount St. Helens National Monument

Facilities:
None at trailhead. The water on the trail must be treated.

46: South Fork Toutle River

0.5 mile scale

forest. Just after some neat cliffs appear on the right, look for a triple-trunked fir tree to the right of the trail.

After 2.2 miles (1.6 since the junction) you'll come to an intersection with the Loowit Trail, which goes all the way around Mount St. Helens. Turn left here and climb just a little more, through a wonderful subalpine area of firs and hemlocks. In August the place will be ablaze with flowers, especially blue lupine.

Soon you'll drop down and traverse an ash-filled ravine with a pond below you. Keep an eye out among the trees down there for deer or elk. After a little more climbing you'll find yourself at the top of a cliff looking out over the canyon of the South Fork Toutle River.

The river, some 800 feet below you, is in the process of recarving its way through the mudflow. The contrast between your side of the canyon and the other side, well within the blast zone, couldn't be more stark.

The trail will now turn downhill, descending Crescent Ridge, for 1.5 miles to a junction with the Toutle Trail—pronounced "tootle." Go to the right here, exploring around the edge of the mini-gorge the river has cut into the mudflow. Then go back to the Toutle Trail and follow it for 1.5 miles through old-growth forest. You'll climb over a small ridge, but the reward is a field of huckleberries at the bridge over Sheep Canyon. Cross that bridge, turn right at the junction, and you're 0.6 mile from the car.

For more information, contact the Mount St. Helens National Volcanic Monument office at (360) 247-3900.

NEARBY ACTIVITIES

If you'd like to see what this eruption was all about, go see the award-winning 28-minute film on the giant screen at Castle Rock, Washington. Castle Rock is at Exit 48 on Interstate 5, 27 miles north of Woodland. You can't miss the theater.

Table Mountain

IN BRIEF

This tough climb has a great reward on top: one of the best panoramas in the whole Columbia River Gorge, including a bird's-eye view of the Bonneville Dam, from a lunch spot atop 800-foot cliffs.

DIRECTIONS

From Portland on Interstate 84, drive 37 miles east of Interstate 205 and take Exit 44/Cascade Locks. As soon as you enter the town, take your first right to get on the Bridge of the Gods, following a sign for Stevenson, Washington. Pay a 75-cent toll on the bridge, and at the far end, turn left onto WA 14. The North Bonneville Trailhead is located two miles on the right—this is the starting point for the longer hike and also has the only public toilet in the area. To go for the shorter hike, continue another 1.1 miles on WA 14 and turn right, crossing under the railroad tracks. Just beyond the tracks, turn right onto Cascade Drive and travel 1.2 miles, to where the road crosses under power lines next to Green-leaf Slough. The trail begins beyond a cable blocking a grassy road that follows the power lines north.

DESCRIPTION

The first part of this hike might leave you wondering why you chose it. Walking under power lines isn't the most thrilling outdoors experience to be had. But this route to Table Mountain's spec-

KEY AT-A-GLANCE INFORMATION

Length:
8.6 miles

Configuration:
Balloon

Difficulty:
Hard

Scenery:
5 volcanoes and the whole gorge from the top

Exposure:
Shady, then open rock at the top

Traffic:
Use is moderate on summer weekends but light otherwise.

Trail surface:
Grass, packed dirt with rocks

Hiking time:
5 hours

Season:
Year-round, but it occasionally gets snowfall on top.

Access:
No fees or permits needed

Maps:
USGS Bonneville Dam

Facilities:
The trailhead for the longer hike has toilets; the other one doesn't. Neither trailhead has water. Water along the way must be treated.

Pacific
Crest Trail

Table Mtn.
3,417'

Viewpoint

Viewpoint

Heartbreak
Ridge

2,000'

Pacific
Crest Trail

1,480'

NORTH

47: Table Mountain

0.5 mile scale

Cedar
Creek

Pacific
Crest Trail

Gillette
Lake

Carpenters
Lake

240' P

47

Cascade Rd.

14

P

47

Greenleaf
Slough

Columbia River

Optional
Trailhead
240'

tacular summit is shorter and much less crowded than the one on the Pacific Crest Trail (PCT), so hang in there. Just step over the cable and follow the grassy road—really just a mowed clearing—under the power lines. After 0.2 mile, turn left (still following the power lines) and cross a brushy creek. At the first tower beyond the creek, follow a trail that leads into the woods on the right.

This trail will go a flat 0.2 mile west, cross a tiny creek, and join an old, overgrown logging road, which (unlike the

trail) is visible on the USGS map. Follow this road slightly uphill for 0.4 mile until you see a meadow on your right. (At the far end of this meadow is Carpenters Lake.) Now follow the road as it switches back to the left, then right again, and begins to climb the ridge. For one mile you'll parallel Cedar Creek on your left, in an area with far more alders than cedars, and then you'll intersect the PCT. Had you started back at North Bonneville, you would have hiked five (admittedly easy) miles to get to this point; by starting under the power lines, you've cut that distance to about two miles.

Turn left onto the PCT and continue climbing moderately through a more interesting forest. There are a few Douglas firs of decent size, but this whole area has been logged, much of it more than once. After 0.3 mile, a side trail leads left to a campsite; stay right on the PCT. About 0.4 mile later, a trail enters from the right; this is actually a route to the summit, but it is insanely steep. Leave it for now, and consider it later as a return loop. The one you'll follow is steep enough.

Around 0.3 mile later, at a large, moss-covered rock on the right, you'll intersect another trail. Turn right onto it and start climbing through the woods. And I do mean *climbing:* Right now you're at 2,000 feet elevation; in 1.2 miles you'll be at 3,417 feet. You'll start in the woods but soon pop out onto the sometimes-loose rock known as scree. A steep, switchback winds up toward the ridge top, then gains it and just keeps going up and up.

When you get to the top, and catch your breath, you'll find that trails actually crisscross the broad summit. Stay to the left for views of Mounts St. Helens, Rainier, and Adams. Go right (toward the Columbia River) for a spectacular view that ranges from Dog Mountain and Mount Defiance to Mount Hood, looking right up the Eagle Creek drainage. Beware that the final portions of this trail literally take you a foot away from a drop of hundreds of feet, and there's no protection.

Those cliffs are part of Table Mountain's fascinating geological history. As you look out toward the Columbia, you can start to make out the fact that the southern half of Table Mountain actually slid into the river, leaving behind the cliffs and narrowing the Columbia to just a couple hundred yards at the most (at the point where the Bridge of the Gods crosses). This slide, encompassing an area of more than 10 square miles, occurred about 700 years ago—basically yesterday in geologic time. It created first a natural dam that blocked the river, then the Cascades of the Columbia, which were submerged when the Bonneville Dam went in.

Now look up at Mount Hood. On the left skyline you can see a ridge leading up to a bump just below the snow line. That's Cooper Spur (see page 51). For a real adventure, hike up that one and look for Table Mountain.

On your way down, you can either go back the same way or do a loop by a thing called Heartbreak Ridge. To do this, as you walk back to the west, stay left, and soon the bottom will drop out. This trail is rocky, steep, and downright treacherous if it has rained recently. But it has the advantage of visiting another cliff-top viewpoint and Sacagawea and Papoose Rocks. Eventually the trail rejoins the PCT at the point mentioned above; just turn left there and make your way back to the car.

For more information, call the Columbia River Gorge National Scenic Area office at (541) 386-2333.

NEARBY ACTIVITIES

Just across WA 14 from the Bonneville North Trailhead is the Visitor Center for Bonneville Dam, a worthwhile side trip to see the powerhouse and, in spring and fall, salmon migrating up through the fish ladder.

Tamanawas Falls

IN BRIEF

A classic falls in a dramatic setting at the end of an easy, beautiful hike. Oh, and it's pronounced "ta-MAH-na-was."

DIRECTIONS

From Portland on US 26, drive 51 miles east of Interstate 205 and turn north on OR 35, following signs for Hood River. After 14 miles on OR 35, and half a mile past the Sherwood Campground, park at the trailhead on the left.

DESCRIPTION

So many people like this trail that even a flood that wiped out half the bridges on it didn't stop them from going up there. Officially, the trail was closed in the summer of 2000, but Oregonians displayed their typical respect for the government by hiking the "closed" trail in such numbers that the Forest Service acquiesced and put in some helpful additions here and there.

The Forest Service intended to rebuild in 2001, but it's best to call the Hood River Ranger District at (541) 352-6002 to see what shape the trail is in. For now, we'll describe the makeshift trail that was put in (by hikers) for the summer of 2000.

The lower part of the trail was untouched. From the trailhead, walk to your right and cross the East Fork of the Hood River on a one-log bridge with handrails. Ignore a trail going up that

KEY AT-A-GLANCE INFORMATION

Length:
3.8 miles

Configuration:
Out-and-back

Difficulty:
Easy

Scenery:
A mountain stream, plunging waterfall

Exposure:
Shady all the way, then open

Traffic:
Heavy use on summer weekends, moderate otherwise

Trail surface:
Packed dirt and rocks

Hiking time:
2.5 hours

Season:
April to November

Access:
Northwest Forest Pass required

Maps:
Mount Hood Wilderness; Green Trails #462 (Mount Hood); USGS Dog River

Facilities:
None at the trailhead; water and rest rooms are available half a mile south on OR 35 at Sherwood Campground.

NORTH

48: Tamanawas Falls

0.5 mile scale

Polallie
Campground

35

Polallie
Creek

Tamanawas Falls
3,250'

East Fork
Hood River

P

48 3,000'

Sherwood
Campground

stream, and instead contour right, parallel-
ing the road for 0.6 mile before crossing
Cold Spring Creek on another log
bridge. This time, ignore the trail that
contours right and instead turn upstream.

In less than half a mile, you'll come to
a rockslide area and a trail splitting off to
the right. The official Tamanawas Falls
Trail went left here and crossed the creek
on a bridge, but that bridge was wiped
out in 2000. The bulk of it was last seen

down by the highway. So the new plan
was to take the trail to the right (a longer
and uninteresting return loop to the
trailhead) until a point where it switches
back to the right in the face of a larger,
older rock slide. It was here that locals
made their new way in 2000. Where the
trail goes right, the people went left and
crossed the rock slide.

This larger rock slide has been here
for a long time; it is, in fact, the reason

Tamanawas Falls in its natural amphitheater

the trail used to cross the creek for a while. The upper bridge that was wiped out crossed back to your current side of the creek, right at the base of the slide. The way to get across the rocks is to stay high and to the right; there's actually a fairly easy way across it up there. If you look to the far side of the slide, perhaps 150 yards away, you'll see two things: a section of railing that marks the continuation of the trail, and several pieces of bright ribbon on trees, installed by the Forest Service when they realized their "trail closed" note at the trailhead wasn't stopping anybody. Just aim for those markers, and you'll be fine. After that, it's about 0.2 mile to the falls.

What makes this falls so special is that even in late summer there's plenty of water coming over it, and also that it's rimmed by basalt walls, much of which are pink because pieces have so recently fallen into the chasm. For this reason, take care if you want to go nearer (or even behind) the falls, as you'll be walking on wet rocks with no official trail and cliffs above you—cliffs that have left ample evidence all around you that pieces of them could come crashing down at any time. These are just little reminders from Mother Nature that we are, after all, visiting her world.

NEARBY ACTIVITIES
Travel north on OR 35 and, in 7.5 miles, turn left and visit the Hutson Museum in Parkdale. It features local history, Indian artifacts, and memorabilia of the early settlers.

Tillamook Head

IN BRIEF

Hiking options abound among the scenic splendor of Tillamook Head and Ecola State Park. You can sample a beach stroll, dramatic viewpoints, and pieces of history on several trail segments, and you're guaranteed to come home amazed. If you make the moderate hike up Tillamook Head, you can even follow in the footsteps of the Lewis and Clark expedition.

DIRECTIONS

From Portland on US 26, travel 74 miles west of Interstate 405 and turn south on US 101. Go 4 miles and take the first Cannon Beach exit. At the bottom of the hill, turn right, following a sign for Ecola State Park. (*Note:* To avoid paying the $3 fee and to add a couple of viewpoints to your day, park at the "park-and-ride" lot at the bottom of this hill, walk up the state park road 0.9 mile, and take a 1.1-mile trail on the left to the picnic area.) After driving up the road two miles, you'll come to the entrance booth. The picnic area is on the left, and Indian Beach is 1.5 miles to the right.

DESCRIPTION

If you were measuring great views per mile of walking, this would be the most efficient area you could visit. Just walking the easy, three-mile round-trip from the picnic area to Indian Beach, you'll get several views of the rock-and-sand-

KEY AT-A-GLANCE INFORMATION

Length:
3 to 10 miles

Configuration:
Out-and-back or one-way with a car shuttle

Difficulty:
Easy to hard

Scenery:
Beaches, cliffs above the sea, historic lighthouse

Exposure:
Mostly in the shade

Traffic:
Use is heavy all summer, more so on weekends; it's moderate otherwise.

Trail surface:
Packed dirt with roots; year-round mud in some places

Hiking time:
1 to 5 hours

Season:
Year-round, but muddy in winter

Access:
To park at Indian Beach or the Ecola Picnic Area there's a $3 per-vehicle day-use fee.

Maps:
USGS Tillamook Head

Facilities:
Trailheads at Ecola State Park and Indian Beach have toilets.

Pacific Ocean

Town of
Seaside

49

P

Viewpoint

Viewpoint

NORTH

49: Tillamook Head

0.5 mile scale

P

Indian
Point

Indian
Beach

P

Ecola
Point

49

Pacific Ocean

101

Park
-N-
Ride

P

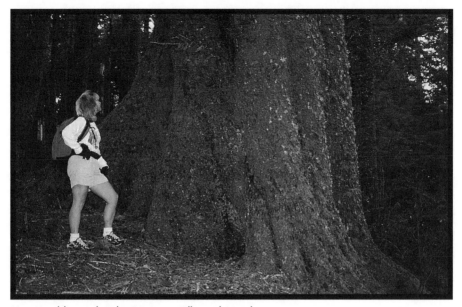

Massive old-growth Sitka Spruce on Tillamook Head

and-water magnificence below. Do as much hiking as you feel up to here, and then kick back on a beach somewhere or stroll around Cannon Beach or Seaside.

First, a little history. On January 7, 1806, William Clark was on his way to see a beached whale the natives had told him about. He and 12 others, including Sacagawea, went over Tillamook Head (he humbly named it "Clark's Mountain") on a trail that forms the basis of the modern-day path. Clark wrote of the view, "From this point I beheld the grandest and most pleasing prospects which my eyes ever surveyed." He also said the coast had "a most romantic appearance." From his description, it's pretty certain that the exact piece of land he stood on washed into the sea decades ago, but you can still experience pretty much the same view.

And if you're wondering about the name Ecola, it comes from the local Indians' word for whale, not anything to do with the deadly bacteria that sounds similar.

From the Ecola State Park picnic area, take a well-marked trail to the north. In its easy 1.5 miles it never gets far from the view, and at a couple of points it's right at the edge of the cliff—though with fences. When you get to Indian Beach, a favorite with surfers, go left and wander down to the sand for a bit.

The trail north of Indian Beach, tougher than the trail south of it, starts just beyond the rest room. After 100 yards, turn left onto a trail which starts climbing pretty quickly. You'll pass another view or two, but you'll also go through muddy patches. After 1.6 miles you'll come to an old road. Turn left for an ocean view from more than 700 feet up, and also for a World War II–era bunker that housed radar equipment. The lighthouse out there—which no matter what it looks like is a full mile from the coast—

Indian Beach in Ecola State Park

was built in 1881 but decommissioned in 1957. It was known as "Terrible Tilly" by the unfortunate souls who used to live out there and maintain the light. Strangely enough, in 1980 it was bought and converted into a columbarium, a repository for the ashes of cremated bodies. The owners make deliveries by helicopter.

Back up the road, turn right to head back to your car, or left for more forest and more views. In one place, not far up on the right, a massive sitka spruce fell over in 1998 but two years later was still being held up by a tree, less than a foot thick, that it just happened to land squarely on top of. Half a mile past the road, and after some switchback climbing, you'll come to a series of viewpoints out to the left, one of which is officially known as Clark's Point of View. Trouble is, a sign marking the spot tends to disappear, presumably tossed into the sea by yahoos.

The official summit of Tillamook Head, 1,130 feet above the sea, is 2.1

miles north of this point. You'll be traveling through mixed forest with the usual views, but my recommendation is to turn back unless you have a car at the Seaside trailhead. At this point, you are 2.1 miles from Indian Beach, 3.6 miles from the picnic area, and 5.6 miles from Cannon Beach. If you did stash a car at Seaside, you're 3.8 miles from there. The trail will continue along until the viewless summit, then switchback down for 1.7 miles to the trailhead.

For more information, call the Ecola State Park office at (503) 436-2844.

NEARBY ACTIVITIES
Seaside is a beachside tourist town. It's worth a stroll, if only to choose between all the fudge, corn dog, and elephant ear outlets on its "Million-Dollar Walk." If you're looking for a little history, there's a model of Lewis and Clark's saltworks (a stove to extract salt from sea water) in Seaside, as well.

Timberline Lodge

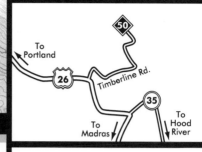

To Portland

26

Timberline Rd.

50

35

To Madras

To Hood River

IN BRIEF

If you spent just one day in Oregon, you should spend it at Timberline Lodge. If you only went on one hike, you should go to Paradise Park in August or early September. But if you aren't up to a 12-mile loop, options abound at this spectacular mountain palace.

DIRECTIONS

From Portland on US 26, drive 48 miles east of Interstate 205 and turn left onto well-marked Timberline Road, two miles past Government Camp. Follow Timberline Road six winding miles to the parking lot.

DESCRIPTION

Timberline Lodge is basically the greatest man-made thing in Oregon. It was built in 1937 by the Works Progress Administration and dedicated by President Franklin D. Roosevelt the same day he dedicated Bonneville Dam. As astounding as the interior is, it's the setting of the place that requires time to be spent there. Only a few peaks in Oregon are above it, and with few trees around, the views are nuts—especially to the summit of Mount Hood, 3 miles away and the highest point in the state, and to Mount Jefferson, 45 miles to the south. In August, wildflowers bloom all over the place.

Let's start with the shortest hike, to the White River Canyon overlook. Follow a sign to the right of the lodge, pointing

KEY AT-A-GLANCE INFORMATION

Length:
12.3 miles to Paradise Park; 6 miles to Zigzag Canyon; 2.2 miles to Silcox Hut; 1 mile to White River Canyon

Configuration:
Paradise Park, balloon; Zigzag and White River Canyon, out-and-backs; Silcox Hut, loop

Difficulty:
Easy to hard

Scenery:
Meadows filled with flowers, deep canyons, glaciers overhead

Exposure:
Alternates between shady and open

Traffic:
Use is heavy all summer long.

Trail surface:
Packed dirt, rock, pavement

Hiking time:
0.5 to 5 hours

Season:
July through October

Access:
No fees or permits needed

Maps:
Mount Hood Wilderness; Green Trails #462 (Mount Hood)

Facilities:
The lodge is a full-service hotel.

Pacific
Crest
Trail

Paradise Park
5,725'

Paradise Park
— Loop Trail

Paradise
Park Trail

Zigzag
River

Hidden
Lake Trail

Little
Zigzag
River

Sand
River

NORTH

50: Timberline Lodge

0.5 mile scale

Mountaineer
Trail

Silcox Hut
7,000'

Chairlift

Timberline
Lodge

50

6,000' Viewpoint

P

Timberline Rd.

To
Government
Camp

you to the Pacific Crest Trail (PCT).
You'll walk uphill a couple hundred
yards, perhaps wondering why you're
suddenly breathing heavily: There's not as
much oxygen up here. At the PCT, turn
right (that would be toward Mexico)
and walk a half mile to the overlook.
If you'd like to do a one-way hike with
a car shuttle, this trail connects (in another half a mile) with the top of the
Barlow Pass hike (see page 22).

For our next toughest destination, go
straight when you get to the PCT and
head uphill 1.1 miles to Silcox Hut.
There seem to be a lot of small trails, but
you can see the hut at the top of the
chairlift, so just head for it. The last part of
the hike is on a dirt road. Timberline
Lodge rents this hut out to groups of 12
or more during the winter. For about
$100 per person, they take you to the hut
by Snow Cat, cook you dinner, then

come back in the morning to cook you breakfast.

To loop back to the lodge, go back the way you came or take the service road under the chairlift. Or, for a slightly longer loop, take a trail that goes right (as you look down) from the top of the lift. It drops one mile to the PCT west of the lodge, in forest broken up by flowered meadows. Turn left and you'll be at the lodge in 0.8 mile.

But enough with the preliminaries: Let's head for Zigzag Canyon and Paradise Park. From the lodge, follow the PCT to your left; it will cross under two chairlifts and start descending slowly as it enters the woods. In 0.8 mile, ignore the trail leading up to Silcox Hut. In 1.4 miles, ignore a trail to the left leading to Hidden Lake (it's a nice lake, but it's 3 miles below you). Just keep on truckin' until, at three miles, you find yourself standing agog at the edge of a massive canyon, with Mount Hood looming to your right. This is Zigzag Canyon. If you've had enough at this point, head back, and you will have done a six-mile out-and-back trip. But for the real prize of this part of the mountain, keep going.

Now, you may have noticed that Paradise Park is actually below Timberline Lodge, making it sound pretty easy. What you need to know, however, is that in the next mile or less, while crossing Zigzag Canyon, you will go down 500 feet and back up 400. Just believe that it's worth it, and press on. You'll cross the Zigzag River on stones (look for the waterfall just upstream), and when you climb to the other side, take the first right (the Paradise Park Loop Trail, 3.7 miles after the lodge) and, yes, keep climbing toward Paradise Park.

This is where things start to get really nice. The number and variety of flowers in this area—lupine, daisies, lilies, and those bushy-looking pasque flowers—as well as the plump sweetness of huckle-berries in late summer make it a prime destination. After 1 mile, the Paradise Park Trail comes in from the left; you can take it 0.6 mile down to the PCT and shorten your walk by 3.8 miles. But those 3.8 miles are flat and filled with beauty, so keep going. In 1 mile things open up considerably, and in 1.4 miles you'll rejoin the PCT. For British Columbia, turn right; for Timberline Lodge, turn left. In 2.4 miles you'll reach the lower intersection with the Paradise Park Trail. Stay on the PCT as it turns left and starts downhill, and in 0.1 mile stay to the right and drop back into Zigzag Canyon.

From there, just retrace your steps and look forward to all of the coffee and hot chocolate drinks they serve at the lodge.

No matter what the weather looks like, even at the trailhead, carry warm clothing on this hike. Mountain weather changes quickly, and Paradise Park is on a normally windswept ridge. For more information, call the Mount Hood Visitor Information Center at (503) 622-7674.

NEARBY ACTIVITIES

Don't let the crowds intimidate you; spend some time exploring Timberline Lodge. Watch the film *The Builders of Timberline* to hear the story of how artists and artisans came together during the Depression to create this master-work. Then get to know the details of their accomplishment, especially the Head House with its massive central stone tower. Don't forget the hot drinks.

Timothy Lake

IN BRIEF

A large and, in places, crowded reservoir in the Mount Hood National Forest, Timothy Lake is known to most people as a place to camp and put the power boat in the water. But for those who love to hike, it also offers some solitude. Not far away is one of Oregon's geological wonders.

DIRECTIONS

From Portland on US 26, drive 61 miles east of Interstate 205 and turn right on FS 42, which is 8 miles past the interchange with OR 35. For Timothy Lake, stay on FS 42 for nine miles. The trailhead described below is reached by turning right from FS 42 onto FS 57 and traveling three miles. For Little Crater Lake, turn right on FS 58 four miles after getting on FS 42. After two miles on FS 58, turn left into the campground and follow the one-way loop to the parking area at the far end.

DESCRIPTION

If you're anywhere near this area, you should at least stop and see Little Crater Lake, one of the smallest but more amazing sights in this part of Oregon. You can also start your exploration of Timothy Lake from this trailhead.

From the Little Crater Lake trailhead, just walk out the paved trail through the big, grassy meadow toward the island of trees ahead. As you approach the lake,

KEY AT-A-GLANCE INFORMATION

Length:
0.3 mile to Little Crater Lake; 13 miles around Timothy Lake

Configuration:
Out-and-back to Little Crater Lake; loop around Timothy Lake

Difficulty:
Easy to hard

Scenery:
A large lake, surrounded on most sides by old-growth forest

Exposure:
Shady

Traffic:
Moderate

Trail surface:
Packed dirt, small stretch of pavement

Hiking time:
15 minutes for Little Crater Lake; up to 6 hours for the whole loop

Season:
May to November

Access:
No fees or permits needed

Maps:
Green Trails #493 (High Rock); USGS Timothy Lake

Facilities:
Several campgrounds in the area have rest rooms and water.

NORTH

51: Timothy Lake

1 mile scale

Pacific Crest Trail

Little Crater Lake

P

Crater Creek

North Arm Campground

Old 1916 Trail

Meditation Point

Timothy Lake

Pacific Crest Trail

Hood View Campground

P

51

Miller Trail

FS 57

Oak Grove Fork

you'll probably think two things: (A) That's no lake, it's a pond! (B) Why did we come all the way out here to see this?

Well, just keep walking. The "lake" is less than 100 feet across, but it's an astonishing 45 feet deep. It's also crystal-clear and a constant 34 degrees. That's because a tiny fault line opened up eons ago, and ever since then an artesian well has been bubbling up to the surface,

eroding away the soil to create this little lake, or pond, or whatever.

If you want to go to Timothy Lake from here, just keep going a few hundred yards past the lake and you'll come to the Pacific Crest Trail (PCT). Turn left on it, and in a half mile you'll come to the intersection with the Timothy Lake Trail. From there, turn left and pick up the loop trail at the point designated below.

If you want to drive to the lake and start your loop there, drive to the Hood View Campground off Road 57. Why? Because, as the name suggests, it has a killer view of Mount Hood, some 15 miles to the north. To start your loop, just walk down to the lakeshore and turn left. You'll pass through the Hood View, and half a mile later, Pine Point Campgrounds; just stay as close to the lake as you can and you won't go astray. After one mile, you'll come to the dam. Technically, you can walk across the log boom on the water, but I would have none of that. The dam is wider and not going anywhere, so I say go on the road.

The dam was built in 1956 by Portland General Electric to control water flow for generating stations downstream on the Clackamas River. When you get to the far end of it, turn right and follow the pavement, then the gravel, through a parking area and into the woods. After all this pavement and civilization, a gauntlet of massive rhododendrons and then a forest of mostly hemlock say, "Welcome back to nature."

After 1.5 miles of impressive forest, take a trail on the right 0.3 mile through an area thick with vine maples, which turn fantastic red and orange in the fall. This trail goes to Meditation Point, with a picnic table and a campground on a peninsula jutting out into the lake. My attempt to find inner peace there was broken up one day by somebody shooting a firearm across the lake—fortunately not toward Meditation Point.

After three more miles on the Timothy Lake Trail, you'll come to a small campground; to stay on the trail here, start up the road and then follow a sign that reads WALK-IN CAMPING. You'll skirt a marshy lakeshore area before rejoining the main trail a few hundred yards later. Just half a mile after that you'll come to the only

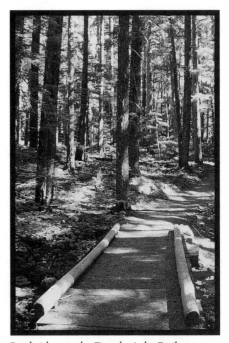

Footbridge on the Timothy Lake Trail

area along the lake that has recently been cut, the advantage of this being that you'll get some sunshine and some wildflowers.

A mile farther along, the PCT comes in from the left; this is where you would come in if you started at Little Crater Lake. To go around the lake, stay on the Timothy Lake Trail and cross Crater Creek on a pretty bridge. Keep tracing the lakeshore, often a small distance to the right. When the PCT cuts off to the left, you stay right, cross a mossy stream, stay right again at a junction, and you're back in campground country. Hood View is 1.5 miles straight ahead.

If you'd like to camp at one of several campgrounds around Timothy Lake, call for reservations at (877) 444-6777. For more information, call the Mount Hood Visitor Information Center at (503) 622-7674.

Trillium Lake

IN BRIEF

A perfect place to take the kids, or just to stretch your legs after driving up from Portland, Trillium Lake is a tiny, friendly lake with a big-time view of Mount Hood. In addition to some short, easy hikes, you can fish, boat, picnic, or just lie around, catch some rays, and feed the ducks.

DIRECTIONS

From Portland on US 26, drive 49 miles east of Interstate 205 and turn right at a sign for Trillium Lake. At the bottom of the hill, stay straight ahead for the day-use areas. The hiking trail, as described here, starts in the second day-use area you come to on the road.

DESCRIPTION

Most outdoorsy Portlanders know Trillium Lake as a cross-country ski area, famed for the terror felt by many beginners on the long hill you drive down from US 26 in the summer. But in the summer the lake is a beautiful, peaceful place to get a little taste of what the Mount Hood area has to offer; and if you've got kids along, they can swim, fish, and paddle in the lake all day long.

To hike around it, start at the day-use area located just before the road crosses the dam at the lake's southern end. Stop here and take the picture of Mount Hood that so many other people have taken; in case you're wondering, that

KEY AT-A-GLANCE INFORMATION

Length:
2 miles

Configuration:
Loop

Difficulty:
Easy

Scenery:
Marshes, lake, birds, forest

Exposure:
Shady except when crossing the dam

Traffic:
Heavy use all summer long, moderate when school is in session

Trail surface:
Packed dirt, boardwalk, pavement

Hiking time:
1 hour

Season:
May to November

Access:
$4 day-use fee per vehicle

Maps:
Mount Hood Wilderness; Green Trails #462 (Mount Hood)

Facilities:
Toilets in the day-use area near the dam; water available in the campground

52: Trillium Lake

0.5 mile scale

square area of snow high up on the mountain is the Palmer Snowfield, scene of summer-long skiing and snowboarding at Timberline Ski Area. Walk along the road across the dam, perhaps throwing some crumbs to the ducks, and ask the fishermen how they're doing. At the far end of the dam, follow the trail to the right into the woods.

In the first part of the trail you won't be right by the lake, as the shore on that side is marshy and filled with tall grass.

So you'll have to enjoy the forest. At 0.6 mile, a short boardwalk goes out to the right for a glimpse of the shoreline. At 0.8 mile, there's a campsite on the right with access to a relatively private spot on the lakeshore. Beyond this point, the trail becomes a boardwalk through a marshy area thick with vegetation. It will seem like you're swimming through the wildflowers late in the summer.

As you round the northern end of the lake, you'll pass from marsh to meadow,

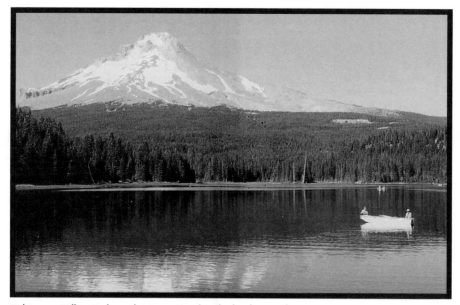

Fishing on Trillium Lake with Mount Hood in the background

with a view of a corner of the lake that's covered with lilypads. Then, coming back to the more crowded eastern shore, there are numerous beaches for the kids to romp on or the parents to sun themselves on. At 1.8 miles (which is also just 0.2 mile from where you started, going the other way) there's a boat ramp and another parking lot. Just beyond that is a dock you can walk out onto (it has rails, so you don't have to worry about the kids). I was out there late one summer day with the sun setting and a few pink-hued clouds hanging around Mount Hood across the way, and some grown-ups on the dock were talking about the stock market and housing prices. Some people just don't get it.

There's one other hiking trail here. Back up at the intersection with US 26,

a sign leads to a 0.7-mile loop through Red Top Meadows. The upper end is at the Sno-Park; the lower end is on the road to Trillium Lake. So if you want to hike it, you'll either have to do it both ways or walk back along the road.

And when you drive out, go around the lake for a piece of Oregon history. Drive across the dam and go one mile on the unpaved road, turn right for half a mile, and then go right again and park immediately on the right near a white picket fence. That's a pioneer-era grave-yard. Across the road is Summit Prairie, where Barlow Road travelers rested the day before tackling Laurel Hill (see page 78).

For more information, contact the Mount Hood Visitor Information Center at (503) 622-7674.

Triple Falls

IN BRIEF
A unique waterfall lies at the end of this moderate hike, but you don't have to go that far to see some fine Columbia River Gorge scenery. You can, in fact, just drive by the trailhead and admire Horsetail Falls.

DIRECTIONS
From Portland on Interstate 84, drive 21 miles east of Interstate 205 to Exit 28 /Bridal Veil. Turn left onto the Historic Columbia River Highway and proceed 5.2 miles to the signed parking area at Horsetail Falls.

DESCRIPTION
If all you do is slow down while driving by Horsetail Falls, you'll be pleased. If that's all you want to see, you should at least cross the parking area and pick some blackberries over by the railroad tracks; they're ripe in late summer. But the great thing about this trail is that the farther you go, the better it gets, and you never have to work very hard at all.

From Horsetail Falls, follow the gravel trail behind the sign describing some of the animals who live in the area. At 0.2 mile, stay right at a trail junction. A few hundred yards later you'll come around a bend and see Upper Horsetail Falls, also known as Ponytail Falls. A popular turn-around spot because it's so near the car, these falls are also a hit with kids because, with supervision, they can get under

KEY AT-A-GLANCE INFORMATION
Length:
5 miles
Configuration:
Out-and-back
Difficulty:
Easy
Scenery:
Four waterfalls, a spectacular gorge, a view of the Columbia River
Exposure:
In the forest all the way
Traffic:
Moderate use on weekends, light otherwise
Trail surface:
Gravel and packed dirt, roots, rocks
Hiking time:
2.5 hours to Triple Falls
Season:
Year-round, though it gets muddy during winter and spring
Access:
No fees or permits needed
Maps:
Trails of the Columbia Gorge; Green Trails #428 (Bridal Veil); USGS Multnomah Falls
Facilities:
None at the trailhead; water and rest rooms are available half a mile east at Ainsworth State Park.

Columbia River

Exit 31
84
Historic Columbia
River Hwy.

P

Oneonta
Creek

Horsetail
Falls

53
140'

Gorge Trail

Viewpoint

Gorge Trail

Ponytail
Falls

Horsetail
Creek

NORTH

Oneonta
Falls

53: Triple Falls

0.5 mile scale

Triple Falls
560'

them and catch some spray. The falls seem to shoot out of a basalt cliff face, and the area behind them is a grotto through which the trail passes. If you get under them, some smaller streams trickle down onto the heads of hikers and dogs. Just don't get directly under the main stream of water; even this relatively small waterfall is extremely powerful.

To keep going, simply follow the trail as it contours around the gorge wall. It soon comes to a brushy area on the right, through which several trails lead

out to clifftop viewpoints of the Columbia River. You can make a side loop out there and work your way back to the main trail as it turns away from the river. There's a network of trails in this tiny area, but they all lead to the same place, so you won't get lost.

A mile past Ponytail Falls, after passing underneath a mossy "weeping" rock face, you'll drop down to a bridge over the top of spectacular Oneonta Gorge. A geologic and biological wonder, Oneonta is worth a visit on its own; from here,

Taking a break under Ponytail Falls

you're looking down into it from the bridge, with waterfalls above and below you. Just across the bridge is another junction; you can loop back to the highway by going right (you'll have to walk along the road, however, to get back to your car) or you can turn left and head up toward Triple Falls. The trail is rocky in places,

but nice views across the way will help keep you moving.

About a mile up you'll see Triple Falls. It's actually just one creek (Oneonta), but it divides into three just before it goes over the edge. It also possesses the rare feature of a large area from which to view it. So take your pictures from here, and then walk another minute or two to a wooden bridge across the wide stream just above the falls. Across the bridge are some nice rocks for picnicking, and just upstream are some pools the kids can jump in, if you've managed to get them this far.

For more information, call the Columbia River Gorge National Scenic Area office at (541) 386-2333.

NEARBY ACTIVITIES

Oneonta Gorge is one of the truly amazing sights in the Columbia River Gorge. You can get about a quarter of a mile into it, but not without getting wet. Even in late summer adults will find themselves wading in waist-high water or climbing rocks to avoid it. (I saw one gallant gent carry his girlfriend through this section.) So put on your bathing suit, and some shoes you don't mind soaking, and explore this official U.S. Forest Service Botanical Area.

Tryon Creek State Park

To I-5

Boones Ferry Blvd.

Terwilliger Blvd.

54

TRYON CREEK
STATE PARK

IN BRIEF

Tryon Creek, Oregon's only state park in a major city, is the kind of place you want to come to over and over, just to see what's going on. Are the steelhead in? Are the fall colors hitting? Are the trilliums blooming? Any beavers around?

DIRECTIONS

From Portland, drive south on Interstate 5 for three miles and take Exit 297/Terwilliger. Turn right at the end of the ramp, then take the first right onto Terwilliger Boulevard. Stay on Terwilliger for 2.5 miles; the main entrance to the park is on the right.

DESCRIPTION

An iron company logged this whole area in the 1880s to provide fuel for their smelter, so what you see today is what's known as second-growth forest. But that shouldn't sound like it's a second-class forest; if nothing else, some of those old tree trunks are amazing! Tryon Creek, a 645-acre park in a ravine between Portland and Lake Oswego, hosts 50 species of birds plus deer, beaver, fox, and a winter steelhead trout run. There have even been sightings of coyote, badger, and bobcat.

There are numerous hiking options that start at the Nature Center, so pick up a free map and pick your own way. For our suggested loop, when you come out of the Nature Center, turn left, walk past the Jackson Shelter, and start on the

KEY AT-A-GLANCE INFORMATION

Length:
The loop described here is 3 miles; there are 8 miles of hiking trails in the park.

Configuration:
Loop

Difficulty:
Easy

Scenery:
A woodsy ravine with a creek

Exposure:
Shady

Traffic:
Use can get heavy on weekends, but it's light otherwise.

Trail surface:
Packed dirt and gravel

Hiking time:
1 hour for this loop

Season:
Year-round

Access:
No fees or permits needed

Maps:
Free maps are available at the park's Nature Center.

Facilities:
Water and toilets are available at the Nature Center.

S.W. Terwilliger Blvd.

Tryon Creek

North Creek Trail

Maple Ridge Loop

Nature Center

P

54

Trillium Trail

Middle Creek Trail

Center Trail Loop

Big Fir Loop

Cedar Trail

Cedar Trail

Red Fox Trail

Tryon Creek

NORTH

54: Tryon Creek State Park

0.25 mile scale

Maple Ridge Trail. As the name implies, this area is home to many vine maples, which put on quite a red and orange show in the fall.

After 0.2 mile, take a right onto the Middle Creek Trail and descend 0.2 mile to cross Tryon Creek at High Bridge. It's worth it to turn right here and explore up the 0.4-mile North Creek Trail, if only for the astonishing fields of impatiens (also known as jewel-weed) and a few places to access the creek, one of them a deep pool at a bend. Return to the Middle Creek Trail and follow it 0.2 mile to an intersection with the Cedar Trail. Follow this trail to the right as it crosses a horse trail (careful where you step!) and then climbs briefly into a more open forest. Keep an eye out for a downed cedar trunk on the right that has obviously been crawled through by many an adventuresome child.

The Cedar Trail crosses the Bunk Bridge, then continues 0.8 mile to a junction with the Red Fox Trail. Turn left here and cross the Red Fox Bridge; if it's winter, keep an eye out for spawning steelhead. Climb briefly to the Old Main Trail, and then turn right and follow it back to the Nature Center.

The nonprofit Friends of Tryon Creek put on numerous events in the park, from day camps, to nighttime hikes, to classes and lectures. To find out what's going on, call (503) 636-4398.

For more information, call the Tryon Creek State Park office at (503) 636-9886.

NEARBY ACTIVITIES

The Original Pancake House, founded in 1953, is located not far away at 8601 SW 24th Avenue. A third-generation family business that has spawned more than 80 franchises in 22 states, this one won the 1999 James Beard America's Regional Classics Award. Go there, get an apple pancake or a Dutch boy, and know what breakfast can truly be.

Vista Ridge

IN BRIEF

A short, easy-access trail to several flower-filled bowls at the tree line on Mount Hood, this hike is surprisingly seldom used. That might be because it's a bit of a drive to the trailhead, but rest assured that it's worth it. You can bring the kids for a short picnic outing or stretch out your legs on an all-day affair.

DIRECTIONS

Plan on two hours to drive from Portland to this trailhead. From Portland on US 26, drive 36 miles east of Interstate 205 to Zigzag and turn left onto Lolo Pass Road at the Zigzag Store. Continue ten miles to Lolo Pass and turn right onto unpaved FS 1810, which is the second right at the pass. After 5.5 miles, you'll be back on pavement. In 1.8 more miles, you'll enter FS 18. Go 3.3 miles and turn right onto FS 16. Go 2.3 miles and turn right onto unpaved FS 1650. Stay left at 2.8 miles; the trailhead is 0.8 mile ahead, at the end of the road.

DESCRIPTION

Exactly why this hike isn't packed all the time has always been a mystery. All you have to do is climb slightly for a couple of miles through quiet woods and you're in wildflower heaven. The bad news is that the beginning and end of this hike can be tedious; the good news is that when you've gone less than three miles, you're basically done climbing for the

KEY AT-A-GLANCE INFORMATION

Length:
6 miles to Wy'east Basin; 14 miles to see it all

Configuration:
Balloon

Difficulty:
Moderate; there's one tricky river crossing to be aware of.

Scenery:
Mountain streams, rocks, glaciers, flowers everywhere

Exposure:
Shady for a couple of miles, then in and out of meadows

Traffic:
Moderate use on August weekends, light otherwise

Trail surface:
Packed dirt, roots, rocks

Hiking time:
3 to 6 hours

Season:
July to October

Access:
Northwest Forest Pass required

Maps:
Mount Hood Wilderness; Green Trails #462 (Mount Hood)

Facilities:
None at trailhead; the closest are at the Zigzag Store.

Vista
Ridge
Trail

MT. HOOD
WILDERNESS

Elk Cove
Trail

Timberline
Trail

Wy'East
Basin

Dollar
Lake
6,000'

Eden Park

Timberline
Trail

Elk Cove

Cairn Basin

day and can choose among four spectacular areas of flowers, meadows, creeks,
and mountain views.

From the trailhead, go 0.2 mile to a
sign and turn right onto the Vista Ridge
Trail (#626). It's not too exciting in here,
and it can get buggy, but when you see
Mount Adams through the trees to the
left, and the trail gets just a bit steeper,
you're almost there. At 2.7 miles from the
trailhead, you'll arrive at the Timberline

Trail (#600), in an open area with
Mount Hood looming right in front
of you. Congratulations: You've now
climbed the biggest hill of your day—
wasn't much, was it? You can go straight
ahead for Wy'east Basin and Elk Cove,
turn right for Eden Park and Cairn
Basin, or go either way and see them all
in a big loop.

But let's turn right on the Timberline
Trail. You'll briefly plunge downhill and

then start contouring around to the left, crossing babbling brooks and admiring more flowers all the time. After one mile of this, you'll cross a larger stream, where logs have usually been placed to make a bridge. A quarter of a mile later, you'll be in Eden Park, which just might be the mountain meadow of your dreams. To preserve the fragile landscape, stay on the trails as they fan out into the grass.

To keep going to Cairn Basin, cross Eden Park and find the trail in the trees as it turns toward Hood. It will climb a small hill, with a view back down to Eden Park, and then pass through a notch and arrive 0.2 mile later in a campsite at Cairn Basin. Here, you can turn right on the Pacific Crest Trail to connect with the McNeil Point hike, which is just 0.3 mile and a tricky river crossing away. Or you can go straight ahead, following a sign for Elk Cove, to complete this loop hike. At the far end of the campsite you'll cross a creek that might be a bit much for the little ones; after that, it's basically a flat mile to Wy'east Basin.

Once there, your car is to your left (go 0.3 mile to the Vista Ridge Trail and turn right) and Elk Cove is to your right. Just 1.2 flat miles away, Elk Cove might be the most spectacular of these destinations; it's certainly the largest, and Mount Hood seems to rise out of its far side all at once. Here, you'll find wildflowers throughout August, huckleberries late in the month, and reddish/orange mountain ash in September. I once spoke to a ranger who had seen elk and black bears in Elk Cove. Give either of them their space, and they won't bother you.

Dollar Lake and Mount Hood

As you head back on the Timberline Trail, before you get back to Wy'east Basin, keep an eye out for a side trail leading to Dollar Lake. There's no sign, but it follows a draw uphill at a tiny stream that's more of a wet spot in the trail. If you get back as far as the Pinnacle Trail (#630), you've gone too far. Dollar Lake (so named because it's almost perfectly round, like a silver dollar) probably should be called Half-Dollar Lake; you could wade across it in a minute. But it's a quiet, lovely spot to contemplate all the beauty you've seen and say good-bye for now to Mount Hood before heading back to your car.

For more information, contact the Mount Hood Visitor Information Center at (503) 622-7674.

Wahkeena Falls to Multnomah Falls

Columbia River

Fish
Rearing
Pond

Benson
Lake

Exit 31

84

Lodge 56

Trailhead at
Multnomah
Falls

↑
Historic Columbia
River Hwy.

56

Trailhead at
Wahkeena Falls

IN BRIEF

Just off Interstate 84 and bookmarked by two beautiful waterfalls, this is the perfect introduction to all that the Columbia River Gorge has to offer, including great scenery, big crowds, and nice, steep climbs.

DIRECTIONS

To park at Multnomah Falls, take Interstate 84 for 24 miles east of Interstate 205 to Exit 31/Multnomah Falls. Park and walk under the expressway and railroad tracks to the historic lodge. To park at Wahkeena Falls, go 21 miles east on Interstate 84 to Exit 28/Bridal Veil. Turn left onto the Historic Columbia River Highway and proceed two miles to the signed parking area at the falls.

DESCRIPTION

When hiking friends come to visit Oregon, this is where I take them first. They get to see the scenic spectacle that is the Columbia River Gorge, they get to view the highest waterfall in Oregon, they get to see old-growth Douglas firs, and they get their hearts pumping—from excitement and, at times, from effort.

You can hike either way on this trail, and park at either falls; my preference is to park at Multnomah Falls (either on the Historic Columbia River Highway or at the Interstate 84 exit) and begin at Wahkeena Falls. I'll explain why later.

KEY AT-A-GLANCE INFORMATION

Length:
5.2 miles

Configuration:
Loop

Difficulty:
Moderate

Scenery:
Waterfalls, canyons, river views, flowers, a spring, big trees

Exposure:
In the forest all the way

Traffic:
Heavy use, especially on weekends. On weekdays and on the trail away from Multnomah Falls, use is moderate.

Trail surface:
Pavement, gravel, packed dirt with some rocky sections

Hiking time:
3 hours

Season:
Year-round, though it gets muddy in spots during winter and spring

Access:
No fees or permits required

Maps:
Trails of the Columbia Gorge

Facilities:
Full service at Multnomah Falls

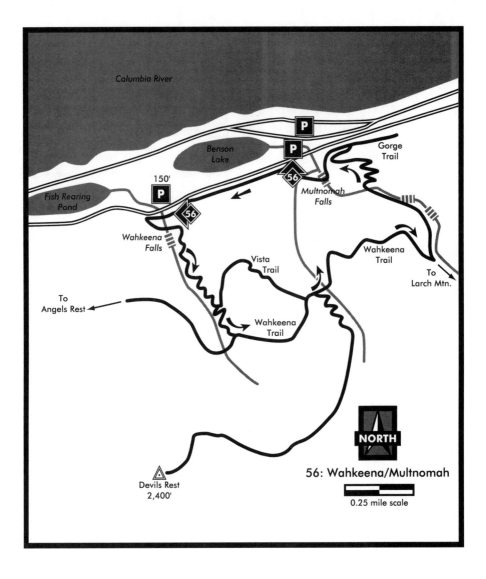

Columbia River

Benson Lake

Gorge Trail

Fish Rearing Pond

150'

Multnomah Falls

Wahkeena Falls

Vista Trail

Wahkeena Trail

To Larch Mtn.

To Angels Rest

Wahkeena Trail

NORTH

56: Wahkeena/Multnomah

0.25 mile scale

Devils Rest 2,400'

To do this, walk 100 yards down the historic highway to the west of Mult-nomah Falls Lodge and take the Return Trail (#442), which parallels the road for 0.6 mile to Wahkeena Falls. Along the way you'll pass under an overhanging rock and be cooled off by a mossy, "weeping" rock wall.

Actually several falls in one, Wahkeena Falls encompasses several styles of falls, from sheer drops to cascades to misty sprays. This creek, by the way, comes pri-marily from a spring up on the ridge that can be visited later by a short side trip. To start the loop, follow the paved trail across the creek and then 0.2 mile up to a footbridge at the base of the upper falls. Take a nice, deep breath of that cool, moist air; your workout is about to begin.

In the next 0.4 mile of graveled switchbacks, you'll gain about 400 feet in elevation; such quick climbs are the trademark of gorge hikes. When you get to a lookout point on the right with a great view of the Columbia, the worst is over. You can rest a few minutes later on a bench at lovely Fairy Falls, sort of a miniature version of Ramona Falls.

There's still come climbing to do; it's just that now it's more gradual and you have the creek and some lovely old forest of ferns, cedars, hemlocks, and firs to take your mind off it. Fairly recent fires took out smaller growth, blackened the trunks of bigger trees, and opened the forest floor for berries and wildflowers to move in. Stay right at a junction with the Vista Point Trail (at 1.2 miles). Then stay left at a junction with the Angels Rest trail.

In 0.3 mile you'll come to a four-way intersection. Take the trail on the left to continue toward Multnomah Falls. The trail straight ahead and up the hill goes 1.6 miles (and up 800 feet) to Devils Rest, which for some reason is 1,000 feet higher than Angels Rest. The trail to the right leads 0.1 mile to Wahkeena Spring, a marshy area that's the main source of Wahkeena Creek, and then another 2.5 miles to Angels Rest.

Continuing west on the Wahkeena Trail, you'll soon start downhill and, in 1.2 miles, intersect the Larch Mountain Trail (#441). This trail (see page 74) connects Multnomah Falls with Larch Mountain. For our purposes here, turn left and head down rock-filled Multnomah Creek. In the next mile, you'll pass several waterfalls in a gorge filled with ferns and large, old-growth Douglas firs.

A well-marked (and well-traveled) paved trail to the left leads 0.1 mile to the top of Multnomah Falls, where a

Top of Wahkeena Falls

wooden platform offers an ego-building view of the camera-toting throngs below. "Yeah," you can say later at the bottom, "I've been up there." This brings me to why I like to do this hike this way. From this point on, especially on a weekend, you'll be among hundreds of people. From my perspective, it's better to move downhill (hence, more quickly) through this scene, arriving at Multnomah Falls and the Benson Bridge a mile later.

The highest falls in Oregon at 542 feet, upper Multnomah Falls is indeed quite a sight. Be sure to stop in the information office at the lodge to see the pictures of various floods and a massive rockfall that occurred there in years gone by. Now for the final reason I like to start this hike at Wahkeena Falls but park at Multnomah Falls: When you're all done, you can get yourself an ice cream cone or an espresso, cruise the gift shop if you're into that, and your car is right there waiting for you.

Trails in the gorge often suffer from slides and flooding in winter and spring, so call ahead to make sure this trail is available: Columbia River Gorge National Scenic Area, (541) 386-2333.

NEARBY ACTIVITIES

The 1925 Multnomah Falls Lodge is well worth checking out, with its skylights and fireplace in the restaurant and old-style stone and wood construction. The food is excellent as well, especially the Sunday brunch. The smoked salmon omelet is out of this world.

Warrior Rock

IN BRIEF

Walk where Lewis and Clark walked on this beach-and-forest stroll that leads to a lighthouse and mysterious ruins on the Columbia River. As a bonus, in late summer there are so many blackberries on this trail that it looks like a grape arbor.

DIRECTIONS

From Portland on US 30, drive ten miles west of Interstate 405 and turn right to cross the Sauvie Island Bridge. The Sauvie Island Market is on your left, 0.1 mile beyond the end of the bridge. After two more miles, turn right on Reeder Road. After ten miles you'll leave the pavement and come to a series of parking areas for Welton Beach, just over the dike to your right. Past that is parking for Collins Beach, which happens to be clothing-optional but is blocked from the road by forest. At 2.3 miles after you leave the pavement, the road ends at the parking area for Warrior Rock.

DESCRIPTION

In the fall of 1805 Lewis and Clark's Corps of Discovery floated down the Columbia River and managed to miss the Willamette River entirely. They weren't fools; the Willamette's entry was blocked from view by the forested wetland, which is now called Sauvie Island. Although much of it has long since been diked, and some is now farmed, about half of it is managed by the Oregon Department of

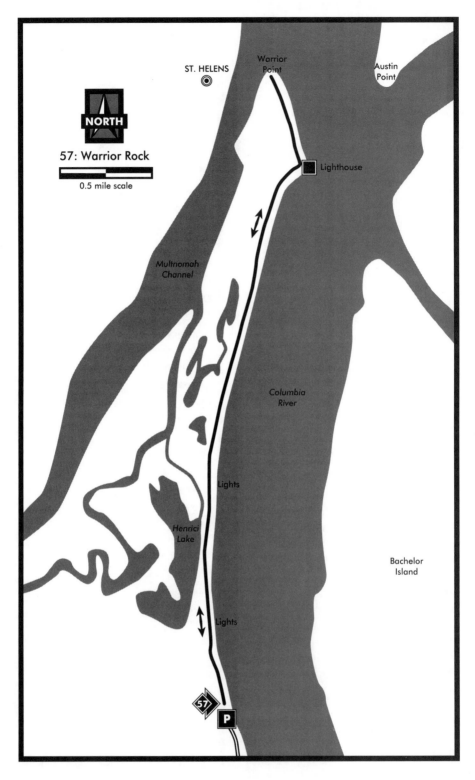

NORTH

57: Warrior Rock

0.5 mile scale

ST. HELENS

Warrior Point

Austin Point

Lighthouse

Multnomah Channel

Columbia River

Lights

Henrici Lake

Bachelor Island

Lights

57 P

Fish and Wildlife. This and the Oak Island Trail are the two hiking introductions to its world of history and animals.

Lewis and Clark, while exploring the island that was the summer and fall home of the Multnomah Indians, actually camped on the beach that lies just beyond the parking area. If for some reason you would like to skip the beach entirely, walk over a low point in the fence at the southern end of the parking lot, and then walk through the pasture, parallel to the river, to the trees. You'll find the road there.

To start on the beach, follow the trail out onto it and stroll along, considering not only what it must have looked like in 1805 but also how quiet it is today. Look also for animal tracks leading from the woods to the water—raccoons, deer, fox, and feral cats are all common here. But those critters mostly move around at night, and if the hunters and fishermen aren't out, you may have the place to yourself.

If it's late summer or early fall when the river is low, you can make it almost the whole three miles to the lighthouse just staying on the beach. Otherwise, go as far as you want, and then look for a place to head up into the woods. Once up on the bluff, you will encounter a trail that once served as a service road to the lighthouse. Follow it through a world of blackberries, oak, alder, and maple. After about 2.5 miles, at a point where the trail is right at the top of the bluff, look to the right for an old shipwreck on the beach. Just a few minutes later, you'll come to a large meadow; stay right for 0.2 mile to the lighthouse.

Warrior Rock got its name when members of a 1792 English expedition up the Columbia (the party that named the river for their ship and Mount Hood for the head of the English navy) found themselves surrounded on this rock by dozens of native warriors. They made peace and lived to tell the tale. The lighthouse was maintained by the U.S. Coast Guard to warn ships of the rock. Speaking of ships, there's a decent chance you'll see an ocean-going vessel, making its way roughly 70 river miles from Portland to the Pacific Ocean at Astoria.

A hundred yards up the sandy beach to the left, somebody cut a perfect little bench into a large piece of driftwood; hopefully, the river will not have reclaimed it before you get there. A few minutes beyond that, at the northwestern tip of Sauvie Island, you'll come to old pilings, which no one can seem to explain. Leading theories are that it was a fish processing plant, a boatworks, or a loading dock for shipping milk from island dairies. Whatever it was, it offers a viewpoint of the town of St. Helens, Oregon, which was founded in 1845—and in case you're wondering why the town and the nearby mountain are called St. Helens, well, the same English sailors who named Mount Hood and the Columbia River named Mount St. Helens for the English ambassador to Spain at the time, a certain Baron Saint Helens. His real name was Fitzherbert; thank goodness they chose his official name.

There's nothing like some useless trivia to think about while you're walking back to the car. Speaking of which, if you stay on the trail all the way, you'll come to the cow pasture above the beach where you started. Just walk across it—careful where you step!—to the fenced parking area and step over the low portion of the fence to your right, next to the hunters' check-in stand.

For more information, contact the Sauvie Island Information Center at (503) 621-3488.

Washington Park/ Hoyt Arboretum

IN BRIEF
A family could spend a weekend in Washington Park and never run out of things to do. The park has a zoo, a children's museum, the World Forestry Center, the Oregon Vietnam Veterans Memorial, a world-class Japanese garden, the Hoyt Arboretum, and miles of hiking trails. The loop described here is only a suggestion.

DIRECTIONS
The best way to get to this trailhead is actually to take the Max Light Rail. It takes you from downtown to the deepest transit station in North America (260 feet—second deepest in the world) with artwork and displays on the geological history of the region. An elevator puts you right next to the World Forestry Center. To drive from downtown Portland, head west on US 26 and take Exit 72/Zoo after 1.3 miles. At the end of the ramp, turn right on SW Canyon Road for a half mile, going past the zoo, then turn right on SW Knights Boulevard. Just past the World Forestry Center, park in the lot on the right. The trailhead is across Knights Boulevard at the Vietnam Veterans Memorial.

DESCRIPTION
This loop hike can be your introduction to and a base for exploring all that Washington Park has to offer. From a hiker's perspective, the heart of the park is Hoyt

KEY AT-A-GLANCE INFORMATION
Length:
Approximately 4 miles
Configuration:
Loop
Difficulty:
Easy
Scenery:
950 species and varieties of plants, with labels on more than 5,000 trees and shrubs
Exposure:
Shady, with occasional open spots for city views or contemplation
Traffic:
Use is heavy on weekends but moderate during the workday or when the weather is inclement.
Trail surface:
Pavement, packed dirt, gravel
Hiking time:
2 hours for the recommended loop
Season:
Year round
Access:
No fees or permits needed
Maps:
The Hoyt Arboretum Visitor Center offers a trail guide.
Facilities:
Water and rest rooms are available throughout the park.

Arboretum (literally meaning "tree museum"), founded in 1928 on land that was completely clear-cut in the early twentieth century. Be sure to stop in the Visitor Center (which is on this loop) for their helpful maps.

Beginning your walk at the Oregon Vietnam Veterans Memorial, follow the trail under and then across the bridge and through a circular series of memorials describing events at home and in Southeast Asia from 1959 to 1972.

At this point, you're in the arboretum—specifically, on the Dogwood Trail. (Each arboretum trail is named for the trees that dominate it.) Follow the Dogwood Trail out of the memorial, and then turn left onto the Wildwood Trail. (To your right is the beginning of this 28-mile "wondertrail"; see page 64).

Stay on the Wildwood Trail for 0.4 mile as it circles to the right and climbs a small hill to a viewpoint between two water towers. Look for Mount St. Helens and Mount Rainier, and then turn left on the Holly Trail and walk 100 yards to the Visitor Center, where there's water, rest rooms, and a mountain of information. Return to the viewpoint and turn left on the Wildwood Trail. In about 200 feet you'll come to the Magnolia Trail on the left; take it 0.3 mile to the Winter Garden if you'd like to cut about 1.6 miles off your hike and stay in the arboretum. For a pleasant, woodsy stroll and access to other Washington Park attractions, stay on the Wildwood Trail.

The wide, flat Wildwood Trail loops out for 1.5 miles, with access along the way to the Cherry, Walnut, and Maple Trails. At the 1.2-mile mark, you'll have a view down to the right at the waterfall area of the Japanese garden; just after that a trail leads down to the garden, the largest in the world outside Japan and a must-see. Just down a hill beyond that is the International Rose Test Garden, with 8,000 rose bushes in more than 550 varieties. Did I mention you could spend quite a while in Washington Park?

Back on the Wildwood Trail, 0.3 mile past the Japanese Garden Trail you enter the Winter Garden, where the Magnolia Trail cutoff re-enters. Just 0.6 mile later on the Wildwood Trail, take a left on the Redwood Trail for an exploration of the sequoia collection. Just beyond that, you'll enter the redwood collection, which includes a specimen of the dawn redwood, thought to be extinct until a few decades ago. This tree was the first of its species in the western hemisphere to produce cones in 60 million years.

Note: If you were to stay on the Wildwood Trail here, you would add a 2.4-mile out-and-back trip to the Pittock Mansion, which is at the top of the Macleay Trail; see page 93.

Back on the Redwood Trail, when you come to a trail on the right marked TO CREEK TRAIL, take that, and you'll be in the middle of the bamboo collection. From redwoods to bamboo—culture shock is now a possibility. The Creek Trail dead ends at a road; pick up the Redwood Trail at the far side, and you'll pass through the larch collection on your way to the picnic shelter. Cross the road, and you're back at the Visitor Center. Turn right, take the Holly Trail back to the Wildwood Trail, turn right on it, and follow it a half mile back to your car.

For more information, contact the Portland Parks and Recreation office at (503) 823-7529.

NEARBY ACTIVITIES

Of all the attractions in Washington Park, the Children's Museum is the newest and hottest. It opened at this location in 2001 and features hands-on exhibits in a "center for creativity, designed for kids age 6 months through 12 years old." Kids can climb, swim, toss balls, and even produce a movie there.

Whetstone Mountain

IN BRIEF

Whetstone Mountain's small, easy-to-reach summit has a big-time, tough-to-beat view. It's also an interesting contrast between the forests as they were and the forests as they are.

DIRECTIONS

From Portland on OR 224, travel 44 miles southeast of Interstate 205, through the town of Estacada, to the ranger station at Ripplebrook. Turn right onto FS 46 and, 3.6 miles later, right again onto FS 63. Travel 3.5 miles and turn right onto FS 70. At 7.9 miles, stay right, still on FS 70. Go 1.7 miles and turn left onto FS 7030. After 5.7 miles, turn right onto FS 7020. Go 0.6 mile and look on the left for a sign to Spur Road 028. The trailhead is 0.1 mile down that road, but if it looks like more than you'd want to tackle in your car, you can park just ahead on the left on FS 7020.

DESCRIPTION

Whetstone Mountain got its name in pioneer days because of a prevalence in the area of a rock that was useful for sharpening knives. As you look at the sign marking the beginning of the trail, you can actually see the summit. Your route will go right up toward it, then turn left below the summit, climb to the ridge, and ascend the left skyline. If it looks tough, it isn't, and the forest on the

KEY AT-A-GLANCE INFORMATION

Length:
4.8 miles

Configuration:
Out-and-back

Difficulty:
Moderate

Scenery:
Old-growth forest (up close and from above), rhododendrons in June, a panorama that takes in several volcanoes

Exposure:
Shady on the way up

Traffic:
Use is moderate on summer weekends but light otherwise.

Trail surface:
Packed dirt with some roots and rocks; one small section of rock only

Hiking time:
2.5 hours

Season:
June through October

Access:
Northwest Forest Pass required

Maps:
USGS Bagby Hot Springs; USFS Bull of the Woods Wilderness

Facilities:
None at trailhead

way up (or the huckleberries in August) will keep you occupied.

The first 0.2 mile of the trail loses 150 feet in elevation as it drops through an area that was clear-cut just over 20 years ago. You'll notice a big difference in the forest as the trail starts up; that's because you've entered the Bull of the Woods Wilderness, a fascinating close-up contrast between a forest logged and a forest left alone. The big-picture contrast

between wilderness and logged areas will be plain later.

After 0.9 mile, you'll come to a rock slide with a tiny pond at the bottom. Note that in this area there is often mud or water on the trail, so consider wearing boots or some shoes you don't care too much about. Also note that at this point you've regained the elevation lost since the first part of the trail. Past the pond, you'll start climbing moderately,

View of Opal Creek drainage from top of Whetstone Mountain

passing two smaller ponds on the left before coming to a trail junction at the ridge top in an area thick with rhododendrons. Turn right here for the summit, which you'll reach after 1.1 well-graded miles and a few steps on rock at the top.

The feel at the top of Whetstone is almost like that of being airborne. The summit seems so small, and yet so high—and consider that there once was a fire lookout here. To the southeast, Mount Jefferson seems closer than it is (25 miles); it's partially hidden by flat-topped Battle Ax, just 5 miles away and about 600 feet higher than Whetstone. To the north, you can see Mounts Rainier, Adams, and Hood—and right below Rainier and Adams,

look for your car at the edge of the clear-cut.

But the exciting thing about this view is looking south and east into the valleys of Opal Creek (see page 128) and the Bull of the Woods Wilderness. It's no problem distinguishing the wilderness from the national forest, is it? Now do the sentimental thing: look toward Mount Jefferson with your hands just to the side of your face, blocking out what has been logged. What you see—the snowy peak, the thickly forested hillsides stretching to the horizon, the roadless sea of trees—is what everything from Alaska to California used to look like.

For more information about this area, call the Detroit Ranger District office at (503) 854-3366.

Wildwood Recreation Area

IN BRIEF

As much an educational experience as a hiking one, this is a glimpse into the natural world of birds, fish, plants, and water that is in fact all around the Pacific Northwest. The crown jewel of Wildwood is the Underwater Viewing Structure, especially when various species of salmon and trout are returning to the area to spawn.

DIRECTIONS

From Portland on US 26, drive 33 miles east of Interstate 205 and turn right at a large sign: CASCADE STREAMWATCH. It's half a mile past the Mount Hood Visitor Information Center. Following the TRAILHEAD sign, drive a mile ahead to the parking area for both trails.

DESCRIPTION

The 33-mile-long Salmon River is the only river in the lower 48 states that is designated as a National Wild and Scenic River from its headwaters to its mouth, in this case, from Mount Hood to the Sandy River, three miles below Wildwood. As far from the sea as it is, it gets several runs each year of anadromous fish—fish that are born in fresh water, go to the ocean, and return to the fresh water of their birth to spawn and die. Although salmon are the most famous of these—and this bend of the Salmon River does get runs of salmon—steelhead do the same thing

KEY AT-A-GLANCE INFORMATION

Length:
The two loop trails total 1.75 miles.

Configuration:
Loop

Difficulty:
Easy

Scenery:
Wetlands, meadows, streams

Exposure:
Alternating between shady and open

Traffic:
Moderate to heavy use on summer weekends, light otherwise

Trail surface:
Gravel, pavement, boardwalk

Hiking time:
2 hours to do both loops

Season:
Open year-round, but the road is gated from November to April. During those times, you'll have to walk in.

Access:
$3 parking fee per vehicle

Maps:
Free hiking maps are available in a kiosk at the parking area.

Facilities:
Water and rest rooms at the parking area; area is wheelchair-traversible.

60: Wildwood Recreation Area

NORTH

250 foot scale

and beyond even that, there are native trout in this stretch of the river.

To get a sample of this natural wonderland, hike two different loop trails, the 1-mile Wildwood Wetland Trail and the 0.75-mile Cascade Streamwatch Trail.

To start the Wetland Trail, start to the left of the parking lot kiosk, where there are rest rooms and free maps available. You'll cross a 190-foot-long wooden bridge over the lovely Salmon River, where in fall and winter you just might see Chinook salmon and steelhead spawning below. Once over the bridge, follow the signs onto the boardwalk. You'll visit several lookouts onto various parts of the wetland: a cattail marsh, an overgrown beaver dam, an area filled with skunk cabbage, and a wetland stream. At each one there's a notebook-style informative display describing the area's wildlife. Also, if you're quiet and go in the morning, there's a good chance you'll see some wildlife. Be sure to take the gravel Return Trail back to the parking lot, if only to admire the size of some 80-year-old stumps and contemplate the fact that they were cut by hand.

The Cascade Streamwatch Trail starts at the same kiosk and takes you on a tour of the world of an anadromous fish. In fact, to navigate the trail you just follow the metal fish in the pavement. Along this trail, you'll visit an overlook of the river, a three-dimensional model of the Mount Hood area, several great picnic areas with grills, and then the fantastic Underwater Viewing Structure. Here, you can see tiny fish most times of the year and try to identify them using the chart on the wall. From late October to mid-December you might even catch a glimpse of an adult Coho salmon. You have a better chance of seeing bigger spawning fish a little later on the trail, when it drops down to the riverside. Look for winter steelhead in January; spring Chinook salmon in March and April; summer steelhead in May; and Coho and fall Chinook from late September to mid-November. In case you're wondering, the Salmon River is closed to salmon fishing; you can fish for native trout at limited times, but it's all catch-and-release with artificial lures only.

For more information, call the Mount Hood Visitor Information Center at (503) 622-7674.

NEARBY ACTIVITIES

Wildwood is actually a full-service 600-acre recreation area, with picnic areas available for rental, ballfields, and a play area. For rental information, call the Salem District of the Bureau of Land Management at (503) 375-5646.

Appendices

What good is hiking without the chance to break in boots, try out a new kind of sock, or see how the latest piece of outdoor wicky-wacky works? If you're looking for gear, here's where to go in Portland:

Columbia Sportswear
911 SW Broadway
(503) 226-6800

G.I. Joe's
3900 SE 82nd Avenue
(503) 777-4526

Next Adventure
426 SE Grand
(503) 233-0706

Oregon Mountain Community
60 NW Davis
(503) 227-1038

REI
1798 Jantzen Beach Center
(503) 283-1300

The Mountain Shop
628 NE Broadway
(503) 288-6768

US Outdoor Store
219 SW Broadway
(503) 223-5937

Appendix B—Places to Buy Maps

Nature of the Northwest
800 NE Oregon Suite 177
Portland
(503) 731-4444

Captain's Nautical Supply
138 NW 10th Avenue
Portland
(503) 227-1648

Oregon Mountain Community
60 NW Davis
Portland
(503) 227-1038

REI
1798 Jantzen Beach Center
Portland
(503) 283-1300

Appendix C—Hiking Clubs

Columbia River Volkssport Club
9325 SW 190th Avenue
Beaverton.
Meet second Wednesday of the month at the NSC Building, 1040 NW 22nd Ave., Portland.

Friends of Forest Park
(503) 223-5449

Mazamas
90 NW 19th Avenue
(503) 227-2345

Trails Club of Oregon
(503) 233-2740

Oregon Chapter Sierra Club
2950 SE Stark Suite 110
(503) 238-0442

Ptarmigans
1220 NE 68th Street
Vancouver, Washington
Meet at 7 p.m. on the second Tuesday of each month at the First Congregational Church.

Index

About the Author

Paul Gerald

Paul Gerald's professional writing career began in the sports department of the much-missed *Dallas Times Herald*. He later worked for the *Memphis Commercial Appeal* and the *Memphis Flyer* before setting out as a freelancer. He still writes a regular travel column for the *Flyer,* and along the way his work has appeared in Northwest Airlines' *World Traveler, The Oregonian, Dish Magazine, Nike.com, Weissmann Travel Reports,* and numerous newspapers around the country. He's also worked in and around landscaping, restaurants, public relations, an amusement park, Alaskan fishing boats, the front desk of the Portland Metro YMCA, and a host of temporary-agency gigs. Such is the varied life of a freelancer.

His hiking life started when he went to a summer camp in the Absoraka Mountains of Wyoming at age 12. His hometown of Memphis never looked the same again, and he has been a trail hound ever since. He's hiked extensively in the Rocky Mountains from New Mexico to Montana, as well as Appalachia, Alaska, Nepal, and Argentina. In 1996 he moved to Portland to be close to the ocean, the mountains, and the big trees.

This is his first book, and he can't wait to bump into fellow hikers using it out on the trails.